The Music of

JOHANNES BRAHMS

In the same series
edited by DEREK ELLEY and produced by The Tantivy Press
(General Editor: Peter Cowie

The Music of Joseph Haydn : The Symphonies
The Music of Johann Sebastian Bach : The Choral Works
The Music of Anton Bruckner

Forthcoming
The Music of Dmitri Shostakovich : The Symphonies

THE MUSIC OF JOHANNES
BRAHMS
BERNARD JACOBSON

The Tantivy Press/London

Rutherford · Madison · Teaneck
Fairleigh Dickinson University Press

The Tantivy Press
Magdalen House
136–148 Tooley Street
London SE1 2TT, England

Associated University Presses, Inc.
Cranbury, New Jersey 08512

Library of Congress Cataloging in Publication Data

Jacobson, Bernard.
    The music of Johannes Brahms.

    Bibliography: p.
    Discography: p.
    Includes indexes.
    1. Brahms, Johannes, 1833–1897. Works.
ML410.B8J28   780'.92'4   75–21260
        ISBN 0–8386–1732–8

        SBN 0–904208–26–5 (U.K.)

Cover design by Mike Carney

Set in 11pt Pilgrim by Five Arches Press (Wales)
and printed in the United States of America

For my wife
BONNIE
who clarifies my judgement
and strengthens my boldness

Contents

Acknowledgement	9
Editorial Preface	11
Introduction	13
Brahms the Man	16
1: Brahms and Music History	24
2: Brahms as Rhythmic Inventor	39
3: Polyphony	70
4: Symphonic Thought	82
5: Brahms the Colourist	108
6: Lyric Melody: Brahms's Attitude to Words	127
7: The Musical Flavour	142
Appendix	175
Selected Writings	177
The Music in Print	179
Recommended Recordings	180
Chronological Chart of Brahms's Compositions	209
Indexes	216
Index of Brahms's Works	216
General Index	219

Acknowledgement

To Carlo Maria Giulini and Bernard Haitink, who have carried on the
great tradition of Brahms conducting represented when I was younger
by Furtwängler, Ansermet and Monteux, and to Adrian Boult, who has
been there all along, for showing me in the most practical and inspiring
way what Brahms's music is about.

Editorial Preface

This series is specifically designed to explore the sound of each composer as his most distinctive feature, and, to this end, recognises the equally important role that recordings now play in musical life. Footnotes throughout the main text contain critical references to such recordings when it is felt that they clarify or highlight the composer's intentions. In the Appendix, these and other recommended recordings are re-grouped in a purely factual listing of catalogue numbers, performance details and any divergencies from the composer's expressed wishes.

Since the aim of the series is to clarify each composer's sound, particularly for the non-specialist, this approach should prove doubly rewarding: treating concert music as a living rather than an academic entity and showing the virtues and faults of its reflection through Twentieth-century ears.

Introduction

This is not a balanced book about Brahms. It is deliberately polemical
in intent. For it is written from a conviction that Brahms is a composer
undervalued, not merely in general, but even by many of his admirers.

On the one hand, his clear links with the past have too often been
taken as evidence that his music is a dead end, of no significance for
the direction the art has taken since his time. My contention will
be, on the contrary, that in the sphere of rhythm alone his influence
has been as far-reaching as Wagner's widely acknowledged effect
on the history of harmony, and that his reassertion of the possibilities
of polyphony and his development of new means for achieving
formal unity have been of no less value to subsequent generations
of composers. For this reason, the principal emphasis of the critical
section of the book is placed on these elements of his style; and because
his music is complex, a great many short excerpts from it are brought
into play to make the argument as clear as possible. I hope that readers
unfamiliar with musical notation will not feel intimidated by these
examples, and that they may even gain some illumination from them
through the explanations given of their relevance and meaning.

But beyond the specific matter of Brahms's historical influence is the broader question of his intrinsic musical stature. "That he stands beside Bach and Beethoven is hardly any more a matter for controversy," Sir Henry Hadow was able to assert over half a century ago, and J. A. Fuller-Maitland, chief critic of "The Times" of London from 1889 to 1911, observed: "As years go on it is more and more generally realized that he is not only among the great writers, but that he must be assigned a place with the very greatest of them all." Yet, for all the fine certainty of those declarations, it has remained an open question how general the realisation is, and there has always been an abundance of dissenting voices to keep the fires of controversy banked.

While Brahms was still alive, as we shall see in the relevant chapter, Bernard Shaw directed some particularly virulent assaults at his handling of symphonic form, and where Schumann had extolled, some later Nineteenth-century composers condemned. Wolf's attacks were bitter, and Tchaikovsky described Brahms as "ungifted, pretentious, and lacking in all creative power." Threading together a number of other comments uttered before Brahms had been dead ten years, one finds accusations that he was "a pompous duffer" with "the intellect of an antelope" and a "tendency to grandiloquence" who was devoid of "charm, soul and personality" and wrote "bad, ugly, dead music"; and in sharp contrast to Fuller-Maitland, the Boston critic Philip Hale issued what amounted to the exact reverse of a rallying-cry when he warned audiences: "Exit in case of Brahms!"

Clearly enough, audiences since those days have taken a very different view, and as in most such cases the dedication of outstanding performers has helped to sway the issue. Addressing the Musical Association of 1907, H. A. Harding asked whether it might not be "that many of those who see little or no beauty in Brahms, and hesitate to place him among composers of the first rank, have never heard his music adequately performed" and argued that there was a need for performers to try to grasp the new elements in the composer's style. "If they are fully conscious of what they are interpreting," he suggested, "Brahms will soon come into his own."

In the orchestral field, particularly, the devotion to Brahms of such conductors as Weingartner, Furtwängler, Walter, Toscanini, Van Beinum, Monteux, Ansermet, Klemperer, Boult, and Bernstein has had its effect. But at no time have the rumblings of disagreement been altogether silenced. Writing four decades after Shaw, Ernest Newman still felt the need to take up arms against those who affect to believe "that none but old fogies like Brahms," going on rather plaintively to remark: "If they would just look around them, they would see that the world is not divided neatly into old fools who swear, say, by Brahms, and young Solons who swear, say, by Milhaud." And in our own time, nearly half a century further on, we have only to note the continuing disparagements of Brahms by such composers as Benjamin Britten, together with small but significant circumstances like the preponderance of dead over living conductors in the list of recordings of even so popular a work as the *St. Antoni Variations*, to realise that the Brahmsian victory is not yet complete. On the very day on which I write, a review in "The Times" of a London cello recital dismisses the E minor Sonata as "a most unattractive work"; and the critic is not an anti-Brahmsian but a man with sufficient interest in his music to have devoted a book to it.

Compared with considerations of historical influence, the question of artistic worth may justly be regarded as a much more subjective issue. Whereas the technical and aesthetic links connecting one composer with another can be established with a degree of factual certainty, since the evidence speaks for itself, in matters of evaluation the task of judgement remains one for each listener's ear and responding mind. Nevertheless, I have tried in this book to marshal the evidence for the view that esteems Brahms as highly as any composer of his century.

Some discussion of other writings on Brahms will be found in the Appendices. But I should say at once how much I owe to Sir Donald Tovey's essays, from which I have taken many ideas (I hope always with acknowledgement), and which are ignored by later writers about Brahms at their peril.

Brahms the Man

The variety of conflicting elements that went into the making of Johannes Brahms as man and musician can be seen in the circumstances of his life from the start. The family into which he was born on May 7, 1833, was a devoted and unpretentious one. His father, Johann Jakob, who was twenty-seven at the time of Johannes's birth, played the bass and occasionally the horn in orchestras and bands. His mother, Christiane (*née* Nissen), was seventeen years older, and had worked as a seamstress before her late marriage in 1830. There was a daughter, Elise, born in 1831, and in 1835 a second son, Fritz Friedrich, arrived.

Johannes's home background was affectionate and happy. But the domestic virtues were maintained against the contrast of the world outside—the squalid, dilapidated maze of narrow alleys and ancient wood-frame houses in Hamburg's dockland known as the *Gängeviertel*. As he grew up, his efforts to contribute to the family budget and ease the pressure of his parents' relative poverty led, physically, to strains that told on even his robust constitution, and emotionally to experiences that were to mark him permanently.

There can be little question that the Brahms parents did all they could for their children. Jakob had no doubt from the outset that his sons were to be musicians, but their general education was not neglected, though poor health prevented Elise from studying. Johannes was sent to a private school at the age of six and transferred at eleven to another one where Latin, French, and English shared a place on the syllabus with mathematical and scientific studies. He was not, it is true, showered with the lavish facilities of a rich man's education, but is is easy to see where the foundations of a lifelong devotion to reading—to literature, philosophy, and indeed all the humanities—must have been laid.

Musical studies began at the same time. Introduced first to the string instruments by his father at the age of six, Johannes began piano lessons a year later with Friedrich Wilhelm Cossel, who soon realised his pupil's gifts and was unstinting in the time and trouble he took with him. A crucial turning-point for Johannes came in 1843, when he was ten. The success of a concert arranged by his father to raise funds for his continued education (at which Johannes took part in performances of a Mozart piano quartet and Beethoven's Quintet op. 16) led to a tempting invitation from a visiting impresario to take the talented young musician to the United States, where he was promised any amount of lucrative touring engagements. The parents were dazzled at the prospect. Cossel saw the threat such a move posed to his pupil's development. When his arguments failed, he decided to appeal to his own teacher, Eduard Marxsen, though he knew he would inevitably lose his prize pupil if the older man agreed to take responsibility for Brahms.

Marxsen offered to give the boy free lessons, and this mark of recognition from one of Hamburg's leading piano teachers finally dissuaded Jakob from his American plans. At first Marxsen shared Johannes's training with Cossel, but in 1845 he took full charge of his piano lessons and in the following year he began to teach him theory. Brahms never forgot his debt to Cossel: relations between their families remained close, and in 1857 he stood godfather to one of Cossel's daughters. In Marxsen, who was a fine musician with a firm grounding in Bach and Beethoven, he was equally fortunate, and equally aware of his good fortune. Their friendship lasted till Marxsen's death in 1887, and by then Brahms had paid his master the tribute of dedicating his Second Piano Concerto to him: not until this, his eighty-third published opus, was he sufficiently satisfied with a work to link it with Marxsen's name.

The seven years beginning with 1846 were the hardest in Brahms's life. There were his piano studies, and conscientious explorations of thoroughbass and other techniques of pre-Nineteenth-century music. There were his own attempts at composition, starting with piano improvisation and quickly going beyond this, in which Marxsen, unlike

Cossel, encouraged him. And at this time began the harsh routine of late-night work as a pianist in a variety of sleazy taverns that was to remain one of his principal sources of income until the early Fifties.*

Brahms gave his first solo recital on September 21, 1848, and the inclusion of a Bach fugue in the programme was an early hint of the young virtuoso's unusually serious tastes. At a second recital, in 1849, he played Beethoven's *Waldstein Sonata* and also introduced one of his own pieces, a fantasia on a popular waltz. By this time, in addition to teaching and playing in taverns and at the theatre, he was earning fairly substantial sums of money by arranging popular salon pieces and composing some of his own for the publisher Cranz under a pseudonym. (This may have been "G. W. Marks," though research has not yet clearly determined whether the pieces that appeared under that name might not have been written by someone else, or indeed by a whole syndicate of composers of which Brahms may have been a member.)

It was probably in 1850 that he first met Eduard Reményi, a dashing violinist who had been a political refugee from his native Hungary since 1848. Reményi introduced Brahms to what was widely believed in western Europe at that time to be Hungarian but was in fact gypsy music. To this period Brahms's earliest surviving works belong, though they were not yet published. He wrote a great many songs in 1850, the E flat minor Scherzo for piano in 1851, and the F sharp minor Sonata in 1852.

If 1843 had been the decisive year in Brahms's childhood, 1853 was the watershed of his career both professionally and personally. Reményi, just back from a long stay in the United States, proposed a concert tour, and the two young men set out on April 19. In May, at the court of Hanover, Reményi introduced Brahms to his compatriot Joseph Joachim. A far greater violinist than the superficial Reményi and himself a composer of stature, Joachim was immediately drawn to Brahms. From now on, until a personal quarrel shadowed their friendship in 1880, the two remained the closest of collaborators, frequently performing together, each submitting his latest works to the other's scrutiny and benefiting from detailed advice and criticism.

Though only two years older than Brahms, Joachim was already an established performer. He gave Brahms and Reményi an introduction to Liszt, who received them graciously at Weimar in June. Liszt was much impressed with Brahms, and Brahms was disarmed by the cordiality of his host, who played several of the visitor's piano compositions at sight. But Liszt's own music was not of a kind that Brahms could

---

*The only real break came with a pair of agreeable summers spent in 1847 and 1848 in the village of Winsen at the home of Adolf Giesemann, who invited him to give his daughter Lieschen piano lessons.

really admire, and besides he was repelled by the scented, court-like atmosphere of the coterie that surrounded Liszt in his residence at the Altenburg. Reményi declared his intention of staying, and the two brought their tour to a premature end.

As for Brahms, he was unwilling to go back to Hamburg with so little to show for his enterprise, and instead he joined Joachim, who had gone on to Göttingen to attend lectures at the university. It was in September, after several weeks in which their friendship developed rapidly, that Brahms took up the second and much the more significant of Joachim's introductions: he went to Düsseldorf to visit Schumann, and their meeting, on September 30, decided the future course of his life.

For one thing, Schumann was enraptured with Brahms's music, and only four weeks later, in his own "Neue Zeitschrift für Musik," he published the celebrated article "Neue Bahnen" ("New Paths") that at once established Brahms—except in the eyes of Liszt's New German school—as the rising young composer of the day. At the same time, the meeting with Schumann's wife Clara—a gifted pianist and a competent composer—was a turning-point in Brahms's emotional development, and his devotion to the couple was absolute.

Schumann sent Brahms to Leipzig with an introduction to the publishers Breitkopf & Härtel. The year of transformation ended with a visit in which he met Berlioz, played his C major Sonata at the Gewandhaus before an audience that included both Berlioz and Liszt, made the acquaintance of the pianist and composer Julius Otto Grimm (another friend for life), and negotiated publishing agreements with Breitkopf for the C major and F sharp minor Sonatas, the songs op. 3, and the E flat minor Scherzo, and with Senff for the F minor Sonata and another set of songs, op. 6.

The year 1854 promised to be one of consolidation. Having spent Christmas with his parents, Brahms went to stay at Joachim's house in Hanover and worked on the B major Piano Trio. But a shocking blow fell on February 27: Schumann, long a sufferer from nervous troubles, tried to commit suicide by throwing himself into the Rhine. Within days he was taken to an asylum at Endenich near Bonn, and Clara was left with the burden of caring for their family: she was already expecting her seventh child.

Brahms went to Düsseldorf to be near her and give what help he could. In 1855 he, Joachim, and Clara embarked together on a concert tour that at least provided her with some financial benefit. Brahms worked on his compositions, gave lessons, and went on other tours. By the time Schumann died, on July 29, 1856, his admiration for Clara had developed into something warmer. What happened between them after Schumann's death we do not know. By his own testimony, he loved her more than anyone or anything on earth, and the bond between them was broken only by her death in 1896, one year before his. Yet from the moment when he might have thought of her as free, a new reserve began to colour his letters. Perhaps she was reluctant to place on a young man, with his way still to make, the formidable responsibility of a large family. Perhaps it was easier for him to idealise his feeling for her than to submit himself to its domestic realisation. At any rate, his attitude to women, and more generally to life, changed from this time on. The young impulsive romantic gradually erected a screen of reticence that made it more and more difficult for him to express his emotions, and as he grew older there were occasional frightening outbursts of pent-up bitterness. To Joachim he confessed that he could no longer think of loving a young girl. There were to be infatuations of varying intensity. In 1858 he became secretly engaged to the singer Agathe von Siebold, only to wriggle ungracefully out of the understanding when it threatened to become publicly known. Bertha Porubszky in 1859 and Hermine Spies and Alice Barbi years later were others for whom he felt an affection that may have been love. But though he often expressed a longing for family life and for children, he never married.

The explanation lies probably in the extremes of his experience with women. On the one hand there were remarkable women like Clara and like Elisabeth von Herzogenberg, who with her husband Heinrich was a close friend of Brahms for many years, and there was his devotion to his mother. On the other was the spectre of his memories of those taverns where he had spent so many evenings in his childhood surrounded by the selling of sex along with liquor, memories that he once referred to when apologising to a friend for one of his more embarrassing tirades against women. There was no way for him to reconcile these opposing images in a lasting relationship without grave risk to his independence, and so he avoided the issue and took refuge in the easier demands of friendship.

*

He was thus left free to organise his life in the way that would best serve his development as a composer. From 1856 to his death in 1897, it was an unusually uneventful life, and not the sort associated with a Nineteenth-century artist. The only dramatic flurry arose from his ill-advised participation, in 1860, in a press manifesto against the New German school. It was a cause for which he had little inclination, since he had been well treated by Liszt, and this solitary political sally can only be explained as an error of judgement forced on him by indiscreet friends. The only major disappointment had to do with his failure to obtain the post of conductor of the Philharmonic Society in his native Hamburg, where he longed to be accepted with the enthusiasm that came his way elsewhere. He had some reason to hope for the appointment in 1862, but instead it went to Julius Stockhausen —ironically, a good friend and colleague—and in the following year Brahms moved permanently to Vienna. There he spent short periods as conductor of the Singakademie and of the Gesellschaft der Musikfreunde, but for the most part he avoided posts that carried administrative responsibility.

In 1857, however, he was still ready for an appointment that took him, for three successive autumns, to the pleasant country town of Detmold, where he worked at the court, teaching the Princess music, conducting the choral society, and arranging folk-songs for its use. After the tensions of 1854–56 he needed a period of calm in which he could start his career moving smoothly forward again. In this, unlike many composers, he was rewarded with great success in his own lifetime. The remaining forty years saw one step forward after another. Occasionally a work would be badly received, as was the D minor Piano Concerto at Hanover and Leipzig in 1859. But even adverse criticism was usually couched in terms that implicitly acknowledged Brahms's stature as a major composer.

Once he had settled in Vienna there was scarcely a check to his progress. At home in Hamburg, however, his parents, who had been growing apart for some time, finally separated in 1864. Brahms made several attempts to reconcile them, but in 1865 his mother died. It is generally believed that the soprano solo movement added to the original six-movement version of the *Deutsches Requiem* was intended as her memorial. Jakob Brahms was a resilient man, and in 1866 he remarried. Johannes had none of the traditional difficulty in establishing cordial relations with his stepmother Caroline. He was conscientious too in maintaining close links with his father: he took him on holiday trips in 1867 and 1868 (the latter to Switzerland), and invited him to come as a guest to Vienna. Jakob died on February 11, 1872, and nothing is more typical of Johannes's character than that he went on doing as much as he could for Caroline and her family for the rest of his life.

By this time a clear routine was establishing itself in Brahms's life. His concert tours continued, but composition was the centre of his activity. He lived quietly in lodgings, and in spite of his generosity to others never developed the habit of extravagance on his own behalf. He was, indeed, quite uninterested in money. Fritz Simrock, who was now his publisher and a close friend, was entrusted with the management of his financial affairs, and when Simrock lost a substantial sum of money in some unwise investments Brahms dismissed the matter as unworthy of any expenditure of thought or regret.

Gradually there developed a pattern of visits—to Italy in the spring, and to resorts in Austria, Switzerland, or Germany in the summer. These holidays were fruitful periods for Brahms, who loved the open air and had always been a tireless walker. A visit to Heidelberg in 1875 brought the completion of the C minor Piano Quartet. The Third String Quartet was finished at Sassnitz on the island of Rügen in 1876. At Pörtschach on the Wörther See the Second Symphony was begun in 1877 and the Violin Concerto finished in 1878. A summer holiday at Bad Ischl in 1880 sufficed for the composition of the *Academic Festival Overture* (written to acknowledge the conferring of an honorary doctorate by the University of Breslau) and of its companion piece, the *Tragic Overture*. The Second Piano Concerto was written in the summer of 1881 at Pressbaum near Vienna, the Fourth Symphony at Mürzuschlag in Styria during the summers of 1884 and 1885. Three summers at Thun in Switzerland were even more productive: in 1886 he composed the Second Cello Sonata, the Second Violin Sonata, and the C minor Piano Trio there; in 1887 the Double Concerto and the Gypsy Songs for vocal quartet and piano; and in 1888 the Third Violin Sonata. Back at Ischl in 1890 he produced the G major String Quintet; then in 1891, impressed by Mühlfeld's clarinet playing at Meiningen, he wrote the Clarinet Trio and the Clarinet Quintet, again at Ischl. Two more summers there brought the piano pieces op. 118 and op. 119, and the completion of the German folk-song arrangements in 1893 and the two Clarinet Sonatas in 1894.

It was in this same year that—thirty-two years too late—the Hamburg Philharmonic invited Brahms to become its conductor. His letter of refusal was written with as much sorrow as Dr. Johnson's famous rebuke to Lord Chesterfield, but with nothing like the same vitriol:

There are not many things I have desired so long and so ardently at the time—that is, at the right time. Many years had to pass before I could reconcile myself to the thought of being forced to tread other paths. Had things gone according to my wish, I might today be celebrating my jubilee with you, while you, as you are today, would be looking for a capable younger man. May you find him soon, and may he work in your interests with the same good will, the same modest degree of ability, and the same wholehearted zeal as would have done
    Your very sincere

                      J. Brahms.

Brahms by now was sixty-one—a frail sixty-one—and becoming increasingly lonely. Of his many friends, he had lost some through estrangement—what his capacity for affection built up, his equal gift of irony sometimes tore down—though the breach with Joachim, total at first, had been partly healed. Others had died: Elisabeth von Herzogenberg in 1892, the surgeon and musical amateur Theodor

Billroth in February 1894. But it was Clara Schumann's death in 1896 that finally—bodily, and not just fancifully—broke him. The news reached him at Ischl, and he immediately started out for Frankfurt to attend the funeral service. But he took a wrong train, missed the service, and after forty hours' continuous travelling arrived in Bonn, where her body had been taken for burial, exhausted physically and emotionally. He was ordered to Carlsbad for a cure by his doctor, but his liver was seriously affected, and when he returned to Vienna in October he was no better. On March 7, 1897, he made his last appearance at a concert, and on April 3 he died. The route of his funeral procession in Vienna was lined by thousands of music-lovers, and in Hamburg the flags were flown at half-mast.

In outward ways, Brahms's life appears such as any composer might wish for: happiness in childhood, friends, financial security, and above all a steady growth of acceptance and fame as a creative artist. It was indeed a rich life, and one enhanced by a breadth of interests beyond that commanded by most musicians. His lack of religious belief troubled others—Dvořák exclaimed, "Such a great man! Such a great soul! And he believes in nothing!"—but it did not trouble him, for he had the strength and the stoicism to do without such consolations. The discordant notes—the growing introversion, the unsatisfied yearning for domestic happiness, the sometimes uncontrolled sharpness of tongue—belie the image of a tranquil, successful man at peace with himself. Their origins lie, as we have seen, in circumstances not of his making, which he coped with honourably and tenaciously. They are part of the complex character of a noble man, and they also helped to create the subtlety and range found in his music.

1. Brahms and Music History

This is a Janus chapter. Brahms faces both past and future, and it will be useful to consider his links in these two directions before going on to analyse particular facets of his musical style in closer detail.

Brahms differed markedly from his great predecessors in his vital concern for the music of the past. It is true that Beethoven had spoken enthusiastically of Mozart and Handel, and that Mozart had turned to Johann Sebastian and Wilhelm Friedemann Bach to further his contrapuntal studies and had produced an imaginative rescoring of Handel's *Messiah*. But the historical gap there had been a narrow one, and in any case, apart from the purely self-instructive aspect of Mozart's researches, neither man could be said to have immersed himself in his forerunners' work deeply enough for his own writing to be much affected. Beethoven's interest in the ecclesiastical modes, exemplified by passages in the *Missa Solemnis* and the A minor Quartet, may be thought of as a more legitimate case of musical antiquarianism. But, once again, it was hardly more consuming than the recurring wave of enthusiasm an ordinarily cultivated modern artist in any period may experience for what he thinks of as the classics in his field.

It was, in other words, an essentially dilettante interest, even when entertained by composers far from dilettante in their approach to the pressing artistic problems of their own time. Brahms's absorption in a musical past extending back at least three hundred years—to the time of Palestrina, and indeed beyond that to the earliest origins of German song—was a radically different attitude for a creative mind. It was to some extent an attitude appropriate to the time: the second half of the Nineteenth century was a period when organisations devoted to "ancient music" were beginning to flourish, so that Brahms was not turning against the spirit of his contemporaries in directing his mind thus backwards. The depth and thoroughness of the absorption was the characteristically Brahmsian thing, for the concentration of his interest was as intense as that of most scholars and more detailed than any composer's until the Twentieth century.

But does such an interest on the part of a composer merely stamp him as a silver-age figure? Some commentators believe, as a general theory, that strong interest in the art of the past is incompatible with really vital creative impulses, and that, historically, the growth of the former is inevitably accompanied or followed by the decay of the latter. Such a view may have its attractions, taken purely as a piece of aesthetic legislation-after-the-event. Examination of the actual effect that Brahms's explorations of old music had on his capacity to make new music suggests that a different, more empirical conclusion may be in order. At the very least, listeners free from schematic tendencies may draw a distinction between Brahms's unfailing ability to heighten the personal character of his own musical language through contact with Schubert, Haydn, Bach, and the earlier polyphonists and, say, the less sure touch of Hindemith, whose recomposition of Weber seems to inhabit a musical world curiously alien to—and far less vitally creative than—that occupied by the best of the music he wrote when he was being more deliberately himself.

It is not only in his music that one can trace Brahms's love for his musical ancestors: there are repeated proofs in his actions and words. He was an avid collector of manuscripts, and amassed a variety of them stretching over several centuries of music. (An especially treasured possession was the autograph score of Mozart's great G minor Symphony.) As early as 1857, writing to Clara Schumann about his work with the choir at Detmold and alluding to his intention of performing Robert's *Zigeunerleben* there, he remarks: "How childishly easy such things are compared with old church music, and my *Salve Regina* [by the Seventeenth-century Venetian composer Giovanni Rovetta] is easy as such things go." "My Ninth Symphony must be like that!" he exclaimed when he heard the slow movement of Haydn's Symphony No. 88, and Tovey relates that one of his favourite maxims was: "If we cannot write as beautifully as Mozart and Haydn, let us at least write as purely."

There can be little question, moreover, that his veneration for Beethoven had a considerable effect on the way Brahms pursued his own composing career. "You do not know what it is like," he said, "hearing his footsteps constantly behind one." Part of the trouble lay in the good intentions of those astute enough to recognise Brahms's gifts at an early stage. "This is he that should come," Schumann wrote of him to Joachim. The support of the most respected German composer of the day, made public in scarcely less hyperbolic terms in the "Neue Bahnen" article when Brahms was only twenty, must have been gratifying. But Schumann, for all the admirable warmth of his enthusiasm for a fellow-artist, was never a profound musical scholar. He was no doubt accurate enough in characterising the piano pieces Brahms had played to him as "turbulent in spirit while graceful in form." Yet Brahms, already a formidable self-critic, knew better than his benefactor the weaknesses of those early piano sonatas hailed in the article as "veiled symphonies"; and his own estimate of the violin sonatas and string quartets that Schumann also referred to may be gauged from the fact that not one of them has survived.

Altogether it is clear that the older man's glowing predictions of greatness carried with them a heavy burden of responsibility. Brahms's consciousness of the exalted expectations thus aroused must have reinforced his innate tendency to caution and his awareness of the shadow of Beethoven; his practice of self-criticism was exacerbated to a pitch that remained, for the rest of his life, nearly pathological. The string quartet and the symphony were the two spheres in which he felt most vividly the supremacy of Beethoven: it was another twenty years before he felt confident enough, in 1873, to release his own First String Quartet to the public (by which time he had already destroyed more than a dozen works in the *genre*), and a further three before he allowed the First Symphony to be performed (after two decades of work on the score)—all this in spite of his general acceptance as a master from the time of the Bremen premiere of the *Deutsches Requiem* in 1868. The final flurry of self-imposed censorship came in the last few months of his life, when he systematically tore up all his unpublished manuscripts. Thus, from start to finish of his composing career, only the relatively small proportion of his output that he considered beyond cavil was permitted to reach the public ear.

If Brahms's awareness of the burden of the past caused him undue anxiety and deprived the world of much music that other composers would have been proud to have written, his sense of heritage had a more constructive side in the positive echoes and acknowledgements he allowed into his published works. The strong resemblance between

the opening of his first published opus, the C MAJOR PIANO SONATA
(1852–3), and the beginning of Beethoven's "Hammerklavier" Sonata

may or may not have been intended, but even if it is unconscious, it is
none the less real. Beyond any question deliberate are the allusions
that he amused himself by composing into the score of the FIRST
SERENADE (1858–59), and particularly into its fifth movement. This
Scherzo earns its name with a witty melange of quotations and near-
quotations from the corresponding movements of no fewer than four
Beethoven works: the Septet, the First and Second Symphonies, and
the "Spring" Sonata for violin and piano.

Handel too—the "Goodwill" passage from the chorus *Glory to God* in *Messiah*—comes in for a cheerful nod in the same movement.

BRAHMS

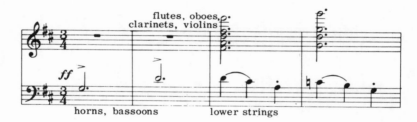

HANDEL

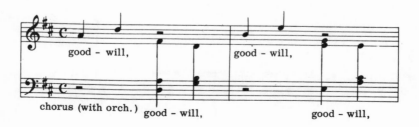

Another choral work, Haydn's *Die Schöpfung*, may be the somewhat more approximate target of a passage in the slow movement of the SERENADE.

BRAHMS

HAYDN

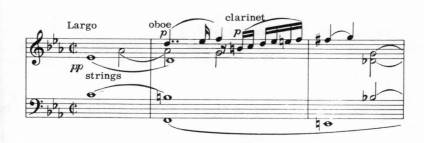

A year later, the FIRST SEXTET shows Brahms up to his Beethoven tricks again, with another sidelong glance at the Septet in the first movement and, more notably, a very precise reference to the Fifth Symphony in the Scherzo and Trio.

BRAHMS

BEETHOVEN

What all these instances make clear is that Brahms was not so much overawed by Beethoven and his other forerunners as to shrink from having fun with them in his own music. In this respect, his practice can be said to reverse the Nineteenth-century trend, moving away from the romantic obsession with originality in art (born of the cult of individualism) and back to the more traditional attitude that regarded musical materials almost as part of a common stock, to be drawn upon at will.

For the most part, specific allusions of this kind disappear after the first phase of Brahms's output. They are replaced by a more profound sense of identification or kinship by which the spirit, and occasionally the thematic matter, of earlier composers' works can be felt from time to time penetrating the entire fabric of a Brahms modulation or theme or movement. With the qualified exception of some of Liszt's studies and paraphrases, which grew out of the very different and entirely practical needs of a composer who was also a virtuoso performer with a busy touring schedule, Brahms's sets of variations on themes by Handel, Paganini, and Bach were the first important works since the Renaissance to take as their starting-points thematic material written by composers long dead. The Handel and Paganini sets combine perceptive re-creations of the sound-worlds of the original themes with equally characteristic elements of pure Brahms in a stylistic fusion of astonishing vitality. The Bach example goes further: more than a standard set of variations, it is a majestic Passacaglia of thirty variations with coda based on a theme from Cantata 150, and in its function as a Finale to the Fourth Symphony it ranks as one of Brahms's most sublime creations. The manner of its integration into the extraordinarily rigorous thematic logic of the symphony as a whole is discussed later in the chapter on Symphonic Thought. Here it is relevant to note the telling modification Brahms made, even before beginning the process of variation, in the structure of the Bach theme itself:

BACH

BRAHMS

Brahms had long contemplated basing a symphonic movement on Bach's theme, but he had remarked some years earlier to Bülow, who eventually prepared the first performance, that "it would have to be chromatically altered in some way" if it was to bear the burden of a symphonic argument.

The result is a movement that stands midway between the pieces formally designated "variations on a theme of . . ." and those many other Brahmsian moments that evoke the style of one earlier composer or another without explicit recourse to a particular theme. Just a few bars after the Beethoven Fifth Symphony reference quoted above, the opening of the Finale of the FIRST SEXTET offers one of the first examples of the matter of Brahms informed by the spirit of Schubert,

and the opening theme of the SECOND SEXTET, composed four years
later, presents the essential topic of the first movement in terms of a
juxtaposition of G major and E flat major that mirrors one of Schubert's
favourite shifts of tonal perspective, this time looking back still further
to Haydn.*

BRAHMS

HAYDN: DIE SCHÖPFUNG

Haydn is a powerful figure in Brahms's background, but Schubert
is an even more potent one: Tovey declared that "upon Brahms the
influence of Schubert is far greater than the combined influences of
Bach and Beethoven." It is an influence felt on a variety of scales, from
localised touches of tonal shading like that shown in the last example
to the farthest-reaching developments of large-scale form. The PIANO
QUINTET of 1864 is perhaps the most copious of all Brahms's work in

* Absolute clarity of intonation is vital to such tonal effects, and is the source of
the sense of authority established at the very start by the Marlboro Festival recording
of the Sextet.

echoes of Schubert, from the major/minor alternation in the main theme of the slow movement

and the reminiscence of Schubert's posthumous B flat major Piano Sonata a few bars later

BRAHMS

SCHUBERT

to the D flat/C conclusion of the scherzo—an obvious evocation of the savage acciaccatura at the end of the Schubert String Quintet.

BRAHMS

strings (with piano)

SCHUBERT

It is this same relation of the Neapolitan flat supertonic to the keynote that defines the tonal angle between the middle movement of Brahms's Second Cello Sonata (1886) and the home key of the outer movements—in this case, the relation of F sharp major to F major. This time the general Schubertian background is reinforced by specific instances in Beethoven (the C sharp minor Quartet), Haydn again (the late E flat major Piano Sonata), and Carl Philipp Emanuel Bach (a D major symphony cited by Tovey). The whole matter of Brahms's choice of keys for inner movements in sonata-style works repays study, and something will be said about it in a later chapter.

Mozart's influence is less often to be found affecting Brahms in any explicit way. When it is there, the sign is usually in the sort of rhythmic subtlety that links the Finale theme of Brahms's THIRD PIANO QUARTET (completed 1875) with the opening of Mozart's F major Piano Sonata, K533/494.

BRAHMS

MOZART

Bach is a much more constant mentor. His voice can be heard not only in obvious cases like the Fourth Symphony Passacaglia discussed above or the set of chorale preludes—Bachian in both technique and ethos—with which Brahms ended his composing career, but also more distantly yet pervasively in the *grave ed appassionato* middle movement (itself a vastly expanded reworking of a sarabande for piano written in 1855) of the First String Quintet of 1882. Handel, whom Brahms studied intensively, is an equally important source, particularly for Brahms's lifelong interest in the rhythmic device of hemiola, by which a basic metre of two beats is varied by the substitution of three short ones or (as in many of Handel's and Brahms's cadences) two bars of 3/4 time are "stretched" into an effect of one bar of 3/2.

BRAHMS

HANDEL: "WATER MUSIC"

Bach and Handel alike stand behind the constant tendency in Brahms's music towards polyphonic elaboration. This is perhaps the feature in his work that is least characteristic of the Nineteenth century. It may, indeed, be more accurate to say that Bach and Handel are Brahms's contrapuntal sources, whereas his polyphonic aspect goes back beyond them to Palestrina and the other Sixteenth-century masters of church music. The distinction between the two terms is admittedly a hard one to draw with any precision: both are concerned with the combination of independent lines in a musical texture. But counterpoint lays more stress on the combination—on the cohesion of the overall texture—while polyphony emphasises the independence. In music that has as clean and powerful a harmonic underpinning as Brahms's, the listener must judge for himself whether a given passage leans more in the one direction or in the other. My own feeling is that, as often as not, the emphasis in Brahms is on the sense of independence, of a number of distinct musics going their ways at the same time.* It is this insistence on the integrity of the individual line, heightened by Brahms's resuscitation of genuine rhythmic freedom in the various parts of the texture, that seems to leap clear back over the previous two centuries to a time before the monodic revolution had shifted composers' concentration from the horizontal to the vertical aspects of music.

This particular backward-looking side of Brahms forms at the same time a natural pivot to considering his effect on later music, for it is in the two areas of linear and rhythmic freedom that much of his potential for influence lies. Brahmsian harmony has produced relatively few ripples in the late Nineteenth-century and Twentieth-century musical ponds. This is not because it is a negligible resource: Schönberg himself has drawn attention to the richness and freedom of Brahms's harmonic language in terms that estimate it no less bold or personal than Wagner's. But Brahms's harmonic inventions, for all their breadth of chromatic nuance, are always to be heard against a background firmly based on the diatonic system of key relations central to the sonata style. They are always functional in the classical, form-building sense. "A false coin," in Louis MacNeice's phrase, "presumes a true mint somewhere," and even when a harmonic touch in Brahms cuts most

---

* Considerations of this kind underlie, to some extent, the choice of recommended recordings to be found in the Appendix. Orchestrally, it is conductors with a gift for separating and clarifying independent textural strands that succeed best in Brahms, where others whose penchant lies more in the direction of vertical dynamism may be better attuned to Beethoven. Thus, recordings of the symphonies and other orchestral (and choral) works conducted by Furtwängler, Haitink, Boult, Monteux, Ansermet and Giulini figure largely in the list while Toscanini and Klemperer are absent from it. The same criterion, naturally and perhaps even more obviously, is among those that have been used in selecting chamber music recordings.

sharply across the traditional harmonic scheme of things, it is the tension between the foreground contradiction and the implied background law that gives the procedure at once its piquancy and its logic. Wagner's interests lay in quite other directions. His music inaugurated the exploitation of chromatic harmony for its own sake, "sensational" in the literal meaning of the word rather than functional, and later generations of composers, likewise unconcerned with the inner dynamic of the sonata style even when they make a show of reproducing its outer forms, have naturally drawn more harmonic sustenance from Wagner than from Brahms.

With polyphony and rhythm the case is different. During the two hundred years before Brahms the basso continuo technique was gradually cementing musical structures into a more and more emphatically vertical configuration. The importance of the chord increased as that of the interplay of line diminished. Except in the most minor composers, horizontal interest was never completely lost. But in Beethoven, whose skill in vertical harmonic procedures and predilection for rhythmic dynamism brought the process to a climax, chordal functions have clearly taken over the control of harmonic space, just as the main beat has gained near-complete domination over more subtle or complex concepts of rhythmic organisation. Brahms's achievement was nothing less than to reassert the possibility of freedom in both these dimensions. "When Brahms demanded that one hand of the pianist play twos or fours while the other played threes," Schönberg wrote, "people disliked this and said it made them seasick. But this was probably the start of the polyrhythmic structure of many contemporary scores." The relatively simple matter of superimposed twos and threes within an overall pulse is only part of the point, and in the next chapter some of Brahms's methods of taking rhythmic emancipation still further are described, but Schönberg's observation is a valuable one as far as it goes. Rhythmic freedom and polyphonic freedom, furthermore, feed each other. Once the tyranny of the all-inclusive beat has been loosened, pulse and line are able to contribute mutually to a further easing of the bonds.

Composers in the Twentieth century have perceived and benefited from these developments to a variety of degrees. I shall be arguing later that some, particularly those whose line of ancestry may be traced back through Schönberg, have taken the dissolution of harmonic pulse a fatal step too far—flooding the market (to continue MacNeice's metaphor) with so many counterfeits that no currency has value any longer. Others have disregarded these new freedoms, proceeding instead along the lines of further vertical specialisation, and, lacking the inspiration of a Beethoven or a Schubert to make the language of regular chordal pulse fruitful, have degenerated into an arid neo-classicism:

Carl Orff is probably the most obvious example of this process, which becomes painfully apparent from a comparison of his crabbed, simplistic *Carmina Burana* with the freedom and subtlety shown by Thirteenth-century settings of some of the same poems.* But the emancipation of line and rhythm has had a constructively liberating effect on some of the best composers of the century, from Ives through Messiaen to Tippett and, in the early and middle stages of his output, Carter.

Brahms's other main contribution has been still more widely taken up and unalloyedly positive in effect. It is his pursuit of formal unification through an unprecedentedly rigorous technique of motivic development. In form as in rhythm, musical vitality depends on the creative reconciliation of apparent opposites. Rhythmically, as the next chapter argues, regularity and freedom are the elements of the creative paradox. In the sphere of form, it is the divergent claims of unity and variety that must be brought into equilibrium if the musical structure is not to be undermined by either incoherence or tedium. This is the principle audiences—and critics—apply when they assess the merits of a symphonic performance: how far has the conductor succeeded in giving due weight to expressive and decorative detail without obscuring overall organic line? In composition, it is the principle that has underlain and qualified all attempts at expansion and diversification from the beginnings of Western music to the dodecaphonic resources pioneered by Schönberg and eloquently (if displeasingly to Schönberg himself) expounded in Thomas Mann's "Doctor Faustus."

In the history of musical thought over the last hundred years, Brahms's recourse to a new degree of motivic elaboration, as a means towards broader and firmer yet more diverse forms, stands equally clearly behind the serial methods of the dodecaphonic and related schools and behind the germinal development techniques of composers like Bartók and Sibelius. The later chapter on Symphonic Thought examines the way it works.

---

* A number of these have been recorded by the Early Music Quartet on two Telefunken discs.

2: Brahms as Rhythmic Inventor

The idea that Brahms's claim to greatness rests pre-eminently on his rhythmic invention may, on the face of it, appear a paradoxical one. At a certain level, the last movement of Beethoven's Seventh Symphony or Wagner's *Walkürenritt* or a Liszt Hungarian rhapsody or, for that matter, a Chopin mazurka epitomises the notion of "rhythmic" music far more evidently than anything Brahms composed. But the level at which this is true is a very basic one.

Rhythm, as a vital resource in music, is not a matter merely of stress accent (of the momentary accretion of weight in the vertical dimension) nor of the horizontal organisation of a number of stress accents (their deployment through the time continuum like so many clothes-pegs on a line). It is, rather, determined essentially by pulse, an elusive phenomenon compounded of both elements and itself dependent on the organisation of harmony and line. In this relationship regularity and freedom have interlocking parts to play. "His rhythm is at the same time perfectly strict and perfectly free" was a phrase actually used of a performer—Henri Neuhaus said it of his pupil, the Soviet pianist Sviatoslav Richter—but what is true of performing is true also of composition, and the rhythmic vitality of Brahms can readily be traced to his establishment of a new equilibrium between regularity of pulse and the elements in music that pull against it. Indeed, since variety under due control never fails to enhance rhythm, it is a whole broad range of balances between the two sides that Brahms deploys. These vary from the minor modification of pulse that approximates to Beethoven's characteristic rhythmic method, to the complex dissolution that makes it impossible for the unaided ear, over a given but precisely defined stretch of music, to tell where the beat is.

In Beethoven, generally speaking, the important musical events tend to take place on the beat, and usually on the main beat of the bar. Even when the phrasing is carried over the bar-line, the pulse survives unobscured, so that the effect is of pure syncopation, or of a rhythmic counterpart to harmonic suspension.

BEETHOVEN: MISSA SOLEMNIS

BEETHOVEN: EIGHTH SYMPHONY

In *b*, which is the subordinate theme of a movement that begins as in
c, the potency of the pulse remains so strong that the ear, rather than
losing track of it, instead takes a moment to realise that the rhythmic
profile of the new theme is identical with that of the old, only furnished
with an upbeat and shifted forward the space of a quaver. An accompaniment figure in the first movement of the SECOND SYMPHONY (completed 1877), and a passage in the Finale of the HORN TRIO (1865), show
Brahms making similarly restricted modifications in the beat pattern.

SECOND SYMPHONY

HORN TRIO

Neither of these instances, taken by itself, could persuade the listener for a moment that the overall rhythmic regularity of the movement in question had been undermined. But the figure from the Second Symphony is not in fact heard by itself. Its context is a passage where the balance between pulse and line changes so radically that the ear is beguiled, or downright deceived, into thinking that the main measure of rhythmic demarcation has shifted. Carefully preparing the ground for the deception over the previous four bars with strong syncopations that undermine the sense of three-beat regularity established earlier in the movement,* Brahms here presents a thematic outgrowth of the symphony's opening material. And the effect of its rephrasing across the bar-line is so decisive that this time, in contrast to the Beethoven Eighth Symphony case, it is the thematic unity that asserts itself, and the pulse that is for the moment hidden.

---

* Boult's recording makes this clearer than most performances by stressing the whole-bar unit even more than the three constituent beats at the start of the symphony.

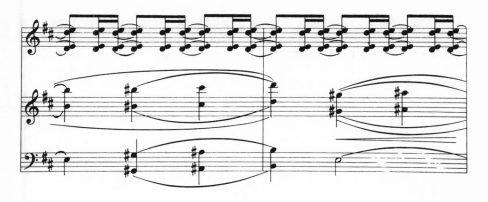

(The melodic sources of the theme are shown in the example in *b* and *c*, which are taken from within the first dozen bars of the work.)

Much play is made in the same movement with varying sub-divisions of the three beats of the basic 3/4 metre. At one point the three crotchets of the fundamental theme are quickened by diminution into quavers, and nothing is left in the texture to mitigate the effect of a sudden switch to 6/8 time.

At another, they are augmented into minims to convert two bars of 3/4 into one of 3/2

or played in canon at two beats' distance instead of three with a similar result.

The latter is the hemiola technique referred to in the previous chapter under the head of Handel's influence. Brahms uses it throughout his *oeuvre*, not only to produce a natural drawing-out of time at cadences and elsewhere in simple triple metres, but also to make the flow of

compound metres like the 6/4 in the slow movement of the SECOND
PIANO CONCERTO more subtle.

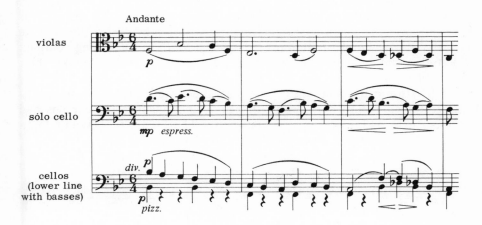

The solo cello phrases the theme firmly across the central division of
each bar, supported at first by the violas, while the pizzicato of the
basses and half the cellos reaffirms the "official" time-signature; the rest
of the cellos can be scanned either way and go unequivocally over
to 3/2 only in the third bar.* Commentators have pointed out the
resemblance between this theme and the subordinate theme in the first
movement of Dvořák's Seventh Symphony, composed four years later,

---

* Much depends here, as in many instances of Brahmsian rhythmic ambiguity, on
the sensitivity of the performers. A just choice of tempo, allied with delicate phrasing
by the solo cellist and the conductor's careful shaping of the bass part, makes the
Brendel/Haitink performance stand out from among the great number of recorded
versions.

and Irving Kolodin has gone so far as to remark that "one wonders how so honest a man and conscientious a musician as Dvořák failed to perceive the likeness." But to insist on the point is surely to discount the part rhythm plays in defining the character of the two themes. The regular simplicity of the Dvořák fits it admirably for its role as lyrical point of rest in a complex, highly-strung movement; the delicate rhythmic balance of the Brahms stamps it at once as something complex in itself, from which wide-ranging musical explorations can take their departure.

Rhythmic dislocations of the sort illustrated above are naturally easier to implement at the start of a movement before the ear has had a chance to assimilate any regular pulse. The Finale of Haydn's Symphony No. 80, composed nearly a hundred years before,

provides an early sample of the trick, dashingly carried out, and in the slow movement of Brahms's SECOND SYMPHONY, as in the third movement of the FIRST STRING QUARTET (completed 1783), it is used to produce a sense of mystery and tension far removed from the light-hearted wit of the Haydn piece.*

FIRST STRING QUARTET

---

* The character of the First Quartet passage is best brought out by a moderate tempo, like that set by the Cleveland Quartet in its recording.

SECOND SYMPHONY

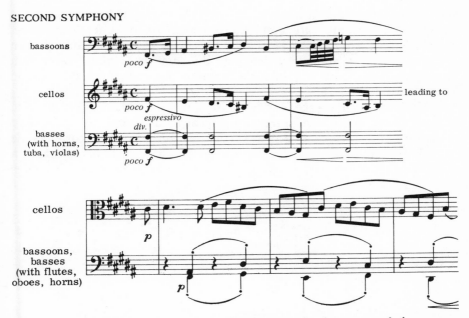

In the Second Symphony case, the fundamental 4/4 metre of the movement, hesitantly asserted in the three bars that separate the two parts of
the example, is called in question again by the steady off-beat accompaniment of bars 6–8.

A radical shift in pulse occurs again in the Finale of the symphony,
this time with even more dynamic effect.

As in the earlier passage, the composer begins the process of rhythmic
sedition with a preliminary paragraph (this time of eight bars, quoted
immediately below) that is itself far from symmetrical, phrasing across
the 2/2 bar-line first in groups of five half-beats and then in threes.
Devices like these, which recur constantly in Brahms, lie behind the
inexhaustible vigour of his rhythmic schemes, and the exhilaration they

produce culminates in a sense of regained security—of haven reached—when the fragments gather themselves once again in a clear-cut re-emphasis of the pulse. To keep such processes straight in the mind in all their complex ambiguity demands the same kind of concentration from the listener as is called for by the higher flights of rhythmic fancy in Indian music.

Closely allied to the device of temporarily dislocating the pulse is the equally Brahmsian practice of repeating a figure—either literally or approximately—in such a way that its successive appearances lie in different relations to the beat. The preparatory eight-bar passage in the Finale of the SECOND SYMPHONY mentioned above is a good instance.

This resource falls midway between the extremes of the cases already considered: it tends to keep the beat clearly discernible but at the same time depends for its piquancy on the contradiction posed by the thematic foreground. The method is exploited with particular inventiveness in the SECOND PIANO CONCERTO. The following example from the first movement shows it in a relatively simple form.

A little later, the potential of this apparently modest device for building and extending form is demonstrated

by a passage that takes an already established theme and converts it by the narrowest of rhythmic shifts into a new one, to be developed still further in the succeeding bars.

The wide variety of effects obtainable in this way can be observed in the second and third movements of the same work.

The latter passage is especially illuminating. Against the background of rhythmic duality already established in the slow movement, these two bars emerge as extraordinarily rich in their ambiguity. If they are scanned in the foreground 3/2 of the main theme, then the melodic notes in the oboe and solo cello parts have the same relation to the minim beat at each playing: if they are heard against the underlying 6/4 of the movement, then the relation to the dotted minim beat is reversed at the same time; and either way, since the repetition is at a distance of four crotchets rather than six, the phrase as a whole introduces a new level of ambiguity over and above the basic conflict of 6/4 and 3/2. Expounded in words, such ingenuities tend to sound crabbed. But it is worth expending some effort on seeing how they work, for what seems arid in the explaining is actually the source of Brahms's wonderful suppleness of phrase and pace.

One final passage from the Second Piano Concerto, this time in the last movement, cannot be overlooked, because it carries the procedure of rhythmic transformation to the ultimate degree of mathematical exactitude.

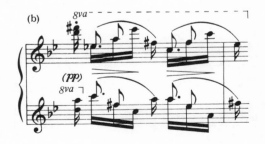

a shows the 2/4 rhythm of the movement as it appears for the last time in its fundamental form before the transition to the coda. In *b* Brahms begins the process of undermining the pulse by phrasing across the beat. *c* starts with the second stage of the transformation, as groups of three semiquavers supplant groups of four, and concludes (after a brief return to fours in the third and fourth bars) with the consummation of the changeover, moving from threes within a framework of four to what is essentially a full-blown 6/8 in the right hand. The effectiveness of the change is underlined when the left hand resumes its former phrasing in the last bar of the example: the 6/8 feeling has taken control to such a degree that the 2/4 figure now sounds like a cross-rhythm—the roles have been completely reversed.

One further factor—Brahms's careful handling of the metronome markings—conspires to make the transition almost unnoticeable in its smoothness. The coda is marked *un poco più presto*, but the metronome figures are more specific: analysing the crotchet = 104 of the main movement and the crotchet = 138 in terms of the constituent parts of the beat, one finds that the triplet quavers of the new section should in performance be as nearly as possible identical in length to the preceding semiquavers. The change of tempo, in other words, should be practically imperceptible. The entire passage anticipates, by more than half a century, the techniques evolved by the American composer Elliott Carter in his Cello Sonata of 1948. The device has been much used by him and others since then, and is known in its Twentieth-century reincarnation as "metric modulation."*

From such intricacies it is rewarding to turn back to some of Brahms's earliest works and to find the subtleties of the mature composer abundantly prefigured. In the previous chapter the FIRST SERENADE was quarried for nuggets of other men's influence. Yet even this first orchestral work—which deserves to be heard far more often—is full of beautiful touches that only Brahms could have brought off. The main theme of the first movement, for instance, sounds artless enough, but its high-spirited statement on a solo horn embodies a cunning shift of rhythmic position.

Two themes in the tuneful Finale exploit a similar resource, in different ways but both with positively Haydnesque wit.

---

* Brahms clearly meant the transition to be smooth, but I have hardly ever heard a performance that fully realised the intention. In almost all the many available recordings the effect is marred either by a jolting change of effective tempo or, where the speed is right, by an uncalled-for pause. Claudio Arrau came close to realising this crux, but it was only with the release in 1975 of Alfred Brendel's superb recording with the Concertgebouw under Bernard Haitink that it became possible to hear the passage played, with absolute clarity, as it is written.

In all three examples the trick, which closely resembles interior rhyme in poetry, lies in the way an apparently simple rhythmic structure based on a four-bar or eight-bar phrase is vitalised from within by correspondences of sound in unexpected places.

The infrequent appearance in the concert hall of another early work mentioned in the previous chapter, the FIRST SEXTET, is equally regrettable. No doubt it is hard to gather two violins, two violas, and two cellos together on the platform in a world where the string quartet has become the standard chamber-music medium. Yet the luxuriant textures that result when the effort is made are glorious in themselves, and Brahms at twenty-seven was already artist enough to keep the cloying effect of over-indulgence at bay. Here again a principal resource for enlivening the rhythm is the shifting of phrase-accents across the beat,

but where the Serenade did most of its shifting within overall patterns of four or eight, the Sextet shows Brahms increasingly absorbed in the possibilities of phrases that are themselves of irregular length. The third of the three main themes in the first movement (actually the official "subordinate theme" or "second subject" in terms of classical key relations) is a wonderfully spontaneous-sounding nine-bar phrase.

Perhaps subtler still is the very opening of the work, where it would be hard to say whether the phrases are of nine or of ten bars' length.

The theme itself is nine bars long as first presented. But the linking figure in bar 10 casts, in retrospect, a new light on the first bar, for when this is repeated in bar 11 it sounds less like a real opening than like the second bar of a two-bar phrase beginning with the link. In consequence the strongest beats of the theme, the second time through, seem to come in bars 12, 14, and so on—which were the weaker bars, rhythmically, in the first statement.

It was to Joachim, incidentally, that Brahms owed the form of this opening as we now have it. The Sextet originally began with the richly-scored statement in what is now bar 11. Joachim pointed out that the modulation to D flat major in the twelfth bar of the theme came too quickly—Mozart, in his *Musical Joke*, had satirised composers who left their key before establishing it firmly enough, and it was a trap that Weber was apt to fall into in his instrumental works—and Brahms accordingly added what appears as the first ten bars of the example.

The sense of ambiguity created by the link-figure itself—is it the end of the first paragraph or the beginning of the second?—introduces another idea that Brahms was to use in a variety of fruitful ways: the phrase that seems to look at the same time forwards and backwards. It can be seen at work in the slow movement of the HORN TRIO, and again in that of the A MINOR STRING QUARTET (completed 1873).

A MINOR STRING QUARTET

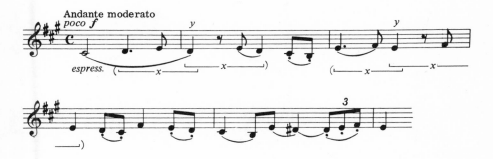

HORN TRIO

In the Horn Trio the piano, picking up the violin phrase in bar 9, neatly conceals its return to the material of bars 3 and 4 under cover of the violin's and horn's concluding bar, so that the theme seems to have stolen back before the listener is aware of it. The Quartet shows the technique operating on the smallest possible scale: not only each of the three-note phrases marked *x* in the example but even each of the single notes marked *y* belongs equally to what precedes and to what follows it, and the result is a searching, self-questioning progress of almost painful sensitivity. (The first eight notes in bars 3 and 4 also echo bars 1 and 2 one step higher, but shifted rhythmically by half a bar.)

When it is used on a larger scale the notion of the two-way phrase affords Brahms a formal resource of the greatest value. The art of transition is central to the art of composing, and this particular transitional technique has a distinguished lineage going back to such precedents as the solo bassoon entry in the duet and chorus *Von deiner Güt* in Haydn's *Die Schöpfung* and the famous, nearly imperceptible start of the recapitulation in the first movement of Mozart's Symphony No. 40.* Brahms uses it most brilliantly at two places in the slow movement of the FIRST SYMPHONY.

(*a*)

---

* A striking example occurs in the rondeau of a C major Overture and Suite by Telemann which has been recorded both by the Saar Chamber Orchestra and by the German Bach Soloists.

(b)

woodwind

horns

strings

In *a* the fifth and sixth bars of the oboe theme are overlapped by the return in strings and contrabassoon to the opening theme of the movement. (An extension of the link between them then carries the music to its first decisive cadence.) The transition to the recapitulation of the main theme later in the movement is shown in *b*, where again, in the preparatory bars, the phrase accents are shifted so thoroughly as to cancel all the effect of the principal beat.* It is in the First Symphony, too, that one of Brahms's most inventive uses of uneven phrase-lengths can be found. The main theme of the third movement (a friendly, lyrical piece closer in manner to an intermezzo than to a scherzo) is a five-bar phrase, followed by its own exact inversion.

---

* The string line here has to be controlled very carefully by the conductor if the *pianissimo* woodwind statement of the theme is not to be drowned. In this as in most other details Jascha Horenstein's Vox recording—probably the finest performance of the Symphony ever put on disc—is exemplary.

b shows how the phrase is expanded to seven bars at its second appearance, and in *c* the further transformation of the second half of the theme into an ornamented six-bar phrase can be seen.

On the smaller scale of phrases a little more or less than a bar in length, a mysteriously hushed string passage in the first movement of the VIOLIN CONCERTO (1878), shows how closely the shifted-accent technique is related to the resource of irregular phrasing.

In a metre of two-, three-, or four-beat bars, any repetition of a five-beat phrase will automatically result in a shift of accent. The same is true of three-beat phrases in 2/4 or 4/4 time, and in all these cases it is the logic and imagination the composer brings to the device that determine its musical effectiveness. It can be seen at its most artful in the FIRST CLARINET SONATA, one of a pair that Brahms wrote three years before his death. Towards the end of the first-movement exposition

the repetition by the piano of a five-note descending scale (itself an augmentation of the figure in the first bar of the example) is enhanced by its canonic imitation at two beats' distance by the clarinet—all this within an overall framework of 3/4 metre. Yet when the passage returns in the recapitulation, the composer embellishes it still further by speeding up the rhythm in the piano part while keeping it constant in the clarinet.*

It is hard to say which is more impressive in this piece of wizardry: the technical skill or the purely musical smoothness and naturalness of the sound. Ultimately the two are the same, which is why it is worth the listener's time to take note of such matters in the first place. Rhythmic devices that sound unnatural do not deserve to be called skilful.

  The last Brahmsian procedure that needs to be considered under

---

* The effect is more readily discernible when the work is played in its original version for clarinet than in either of the string instrument arrangements. The more vibrant tone of the strings makes it harder for the piano to convey this particular point without great restraint on the string player's part, though the recording of the viola version by Pinchas Zukerman and Daniel Barenboim shows—by contrast with the otherwise good performance by Walter Trampler and Mieczysław Horszowski—that the trick can be done.

the head of rhythmic invention is another consequence of the absorption with three-against-two patterns, already traced in the first movement of the Second Symphony and the slow movement of the Second Piano Concerto—an absorption that amounts almost to an obsession throughout Brahms's career. In this new context tension between conflicting patterns expresses itself in an explicit change of metre.

This happens often in Brahms's scherzos. The change is effected clearly enough by the notation in the scherzo of the HORN TRIO without recourse to a new time signature, but that of the PIANO QUINTET changes no fewer than thirteen times (taking the *da capo* into account) between 6/8 and 2/4.

HORN TRIO

PIANO QUINTET

In addition to changes in the internal structure of the bar or beat, the wider grouping of beats is sometimes modified by a change of time signature, as in the Scherzo of the THIRD PIANO QUARTET and the Finale of the First Piano Sonata (1853), which oscillate between 6/8 and 9/8; and the Finale of the CLARINET TRIO (1891) embodies changes in both internal and wider beat pattern within the space of a few bars.*

CLARINET TRIO

* A less well-known instance is *Es rauschet das Wasser*, the third of the Four Duets for alto, baritone, and piano, op. 28, which begins with a long, gently flowing passage in common (4/4) time, but develops into a subtle patchwork of 4/4, 6/4, and 3/4 by the time it is finished. The recorded performance by Janet Baker, Dietrich Fischer-Dieskau, and Daniel Barenboim beautifully captures the freedom of the music's flow, though oddly missing the effect of the 4/4 bar that links the last segments of 3/4 and 6/4 time.

THIRD PIANO QUARTET

Like most of the techniques examined, specific changes of time are not only used by Brahms on the purely "local" plane. In some works, most strikingly the First and Third String Quartets, they play a central determining role in the organisation of the musical argument. The opening allegro of the FIRST QUARTET makes much play with regroupings of its basic three minim beats in sets of two

so that the effect is of inexorable logic when the movement debouches squarely into 2/2 for its coda. The symphonic progression continues with the reshaping of thematic material, by way of the opening of the slow movement, into the main theme of the Finale, which blends the manner of the first movement with the substance of the second and at the same time confirms the overall trend away from three-beat patterns towards twos.

The opening of the third movement, already quoted on page 46, reveals an intermediate stage of the process, especially if its very first phrase is compared with the melodic line in the third bar of *b* in this example.

In the THIRD QUARTET (completed 1876) the interpenetration of twos and threes dominates the first movement more intensively still, giving rise to constant shifts and to a wealth of rhythmic cross-fertilisation that keeps the music and the listener always on their toes.*

---

*The crisply classical style of the Fine Arts Quartet's performance is particularly successful in capturing the elastic vigour of these rhythmic *jeux d'esprit*.

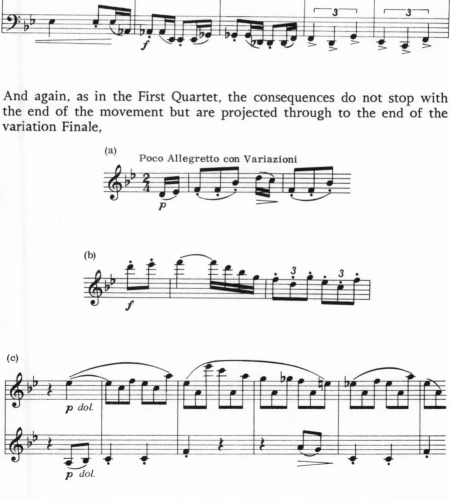

And again, as in the First Quartet, the consequences do not stop with the end of the movement but are projected through to the end of the variation Finale, whose theme, shown in *a*, is eventually welded in the subtlest possible manner with the main themes (and rhythms) of the first movement.

Behind all the shifts and expansions and contractions of pulse in the examples considered above, Brahms's music never loses its sense of purpose and direction. This is ultimately because, as a master contrapuntist with the roots of his linear style firmly planted in the Sixteenth century, he keeps his bass line lucidly and muscularly mobile. Almost always, when a listener feels that a piece of music lacks drive (that it "doesn't seem to go anywhere"), the crucial cause can be found in a sense of indeterminacy, a lack of logic, in the bass.

This is why much Twentieth-century music, especially that written in twelve-note and other pan-chromatic techniques, fails to achieve momentum even when it is clearly aiming for it. (Some recent music that is *deliberately* static cannot justly be criticised along such lines.) When Brahms's liberating rhythmic devices were adopted by Schönberg and his followers they lost their effect, for any amount of metrical irregularity can only attain to real rhythmic freedom if some degree of regularity has been established in the first place. You cannot depart from a pulse that does not exist. The dodecaphonists tried to exploit the departures without providing the pulse, essentially because their attempt to render all the twelve semitones on the chromatic scale democratically equal had resulted in the harmonic neutralisation of the bass line. It can hardly be a coincidence that the one work of Schönberg's that Wilhelm Furtwängler really identified himself with—he conducted its first performance—was the *Variations for Orchestra*. This is also the work in which Schönberg, though the repetition and dance-like treatment of the bass, comes closest to establishing a true harmonic pulse.*

On a theoretical level, the seed of Schönberg's problem can be found in the nature of his views on "musical prose," which he enthusiastically designates, in his essay "Brahms the Progressive," as Brahms's goal. The tell-tale flaw in his thinking emerges in his discussion of the transition from main to subordinate theme in the first movement of Mozart's D minor Quartet. The passage, according to Schönberg, "certainly deserves the qualification of musical prose," and he goes on to

---

* Furtwängler's supremacy as a Brahms conductor derived in part, as his recordings demonstrate, from his unfailing care in according the bass line its due weight. This factor emerges vividly, even through the medium of relatively dim sound reproduction, in his recordings of the four symphonies. It is a central element, too, in Bernard Haitink's high and still growing stature as a Brahms conductor, as clearly evident in his performance of the Violin Concerto with Herman Krebbers as in his symphony recordings. Haitink's performance of the Third Symphony is equally impressive in this respect, but has been omitted from the list of recommended recordings because it seems to me to break up the 6/4 metre of the first movement with too chunkily emphatic a subdivision of the beat into its constituent parts.

locate its "prose-like" quality in "the unexcelled freedom of its rhythm and the perfect independence from formal symmetry." The rhythm of the passage, certainly, is unexcelled in its freedom. But to speak of "perfect independence from formal symmetry" is to beg the vital question: it ignores the link between Mozart's superbly crafted musical foreground and the underlying regularity in which the freedom has its frame of reference, and without which it would be mere anarchy. It is to such abandonments of music's background frames of reference that we owe the tedious succession of those Twentieth-century—and Nineteenth-century—works whose frantic switches from *adagio* to *presto* and back have no effect on their actual progress, because at no time is the music moving at any particular speed whatsoever. With Brahms the pulse is never far below the edge of the listener's consciousness, and so the pull against it always tells.

3: Polyphony

Counterpoint and polyphony are not matters just of writing one fugue after another. Linear freedom in Brahms is a resource that informs and aerates the entire warp of the musical texture, rather than being pressed into service on an occasional basis as a special effect. Indeed, Brahms wrote—or at least admitted into his published works—fewer "official" fugues than most of the great composers. The Handel Variations of 1861 culminate in an exuberant giant of the *genre*, and the Finale of the First Cello Sonata, completed four years later, is another, slightly less ambitious one. Earlier, there are a group of organ fugues and a prominent fugato episode in the Finale of the First Piano Concerto. But apart from obvious exceptions like the fugues in the *Deutsches Requiem*, Brahms's later music shows him turning away from formal fugal methods. In the same degree he grew increasingly wary of ingenuities like the somewhat self-advertising canons in the solo piano Schumann Variations (1854), one of which provoked him later in life to a pointed marginal question-mark. The elaborately contrapuntal Eleven Chorale Preludes published posthumously do not really contradict the trend, since this final opus is an exceptional case, consciously valedictory in its return to the spirit of Bach.

If Brahms's handling of polyphony grew more flexible as his language matured, his absorption in it certainly did not abate. It was one of his basic tools for revitalising the sonata style, and at the same time the most tangible fruit of his enthusiasm for pre-classical music. This was a preoccupation that gripped him early, as much through his own predilections as through his good fortune in being accepted as a piano pupil, at the age of ten, by Eduard Marxsen, himself a dedicated student of Bach and his forebears. So it is not surprising that Brahms's style, as Tovey puts it, "was from the outset almost evenly balanced between the most dramatic sonata form and the highest polyphony."

In considering the case for Brahms as a rhythmic innovator of unsurpassed originality, we have already had occasion to look at a number of passages that could equally well illustrate his polyphonic gifts. The two stylistic elements are inextricably linked: emancipation of pulse reinforces freedom of line, since it is clearly much easier for one strand in a musical texture to assert its independence when rhythmic variety has dispersed the vertical correspondence of note-value associated with a simple controlling beat. But there are also instances where the contrapuntal interest is relatively unaffected by rhythmic factors.

Here again the FIRST SERENADE (1858–59) proves to be a compendium of the essential Brahms, and two passages in the first movement suffice to demonstrate how quickly his technique acquired that immaculate appearance of ease without which contrapuntal effects are no more enjoyable than sore thumbs. The first pits violins against cellos, basses, and bassoons in close canon, the two lines shaded in parallel thirds, while the violas mirror the violin figure in approximate inversion. In the second, the imitation of the first violin theme by second violins and violas at a bar-and-a-half's distance is merely an embellishment, and the chief interest lies in the contrary motion of first violins and cellos.*

---

* The clarity of interweaving lines must have been even more marked in the original nonet version of the score, and it benefits from the use of chamber orchestral forces in Anshel Brusilow's recording—an extraordinarily beautiful performance well worth seeking out.

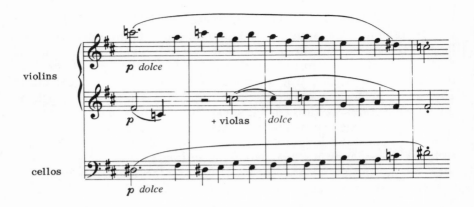

For all their smoothness and euphony, there remains perhaps in these examples a trace of indulgence in ingenuity for its own sake, or at least a sense that the composer is exulting consciously in his newly-won freedom of movement. By the time of the G MINOR PIANO QUARTET (1861), canonic imitation has been absorbed so thoroughly into his language that no sign of self-consciousness remains.

The last movement of this Quartet, a gypsy rondo (*Rondo alla zingarese*) that shocked Brahms's more serious-minded admirers, is probably his most determinedly homophonic movement with its strenuously juxta-posed blocks of dance material. Yet even here, as *b* in the example shows, Brahms could not resist a brief flight of polyphonic fancy, this time as a well-judged touch of relief from the untypical regularity of pulse that pervades the rest of the music.

 Closer to *a* above—since it appears as part of a seamless develop-ment process, rather than as a moment of sharp contrast—is a canonic passage in the first movement of the very next work, the A MAJOR PIANO QUARTET.

Coming near the end of a long movement, this simple, but telling intensification of texture has the appropriate effect of summing up the tone of undulating rhythmic instability from which the music takes its slightly teasing character—the original form of the theme is shown in *b* of the example.

 Owing no doubt to his deliberate policy of suppressing all but his most perfectly finished works, Brahms's surviving music affords no opportunity to observe significant stages in the growth of his polyphonic skill. The technique seems to spring forth fully formed, like Athene in her armour. What increases, as his career progresses, is only the degree of freedom in its application and of euphony or dramatic force in the result—qualities that would be judged remarkable enough in the earliest works if the later ones had not provided a stiffer criterion of mastery.

 Insofar as individual steps in this progress can be measured, the PIANO QUINTET represents as substantial a move forward as any of Brahms's works. There is a perceptible growth of freedom, and thus of symphonic power, at many junctures in the first movement, among them an impressively plastic polyphonic expansion of a brief piano phrase, and a tense canon by inversion in the development section.

Nor is the force of expression relaxed in the Finale, where the deceptive innocence of the main theme scarcely prepares the listener for the frightening intensity of its canonic treatment in the course of the movement.

The sense of effortless flexibility is maintained in the SECOND SEXTET. One vigorous imitative development in the first movement achieves a new level of piquancy by mischievously contracting the five-beat gap between its first two entries to two beats at the repetition eight bars later, exercising the ear in the process with a not-so-incidental semitone clash.

But it is for the sheer euphony of its polyphonic writing that this sunny movement, unusually loose-limbed in phrasing for Brahms, is especially notable. It emulates the richness of the First Sextet, but with a sharper linear edge.

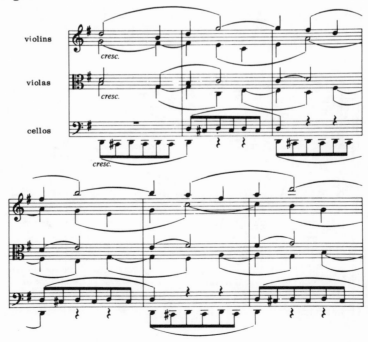

In its spacious counterpoint, the development section, which opens as in the example below, is perhaps the only place in his entire *oeuvre* where Brahms sounds at all like Bruckner.

With its three big fugal sections, the DEUTSCHES REQUIEM is sometimes regarded as a backward step towards formalism on Brahms's part.
But whereas critics often profess to find *Der Gerechten Seelen sind in
Gottes Hand* arid, its effect in the concert hall can be exhilarating: the
archaic *alla breve* bars and the unremitting pedal D in the bass may
look dry on paper (see plate 3), but they contribute to the over-
whelming physical impact of the music. Even at its most apparently
old-fashioned and churchy, the *Die Erlöseten des Herrn* fugue is full of
expressive sap, and *Herr, du bist würdig*, stretching out in a seemingly
infinite chain of striding sequences on the words *zu nehmen Preis und
Ehre*, is the mightiest Nineteenth-century fugue outside the last works
of Beethoven.

"HERR, DU BIST WÜRDIG"

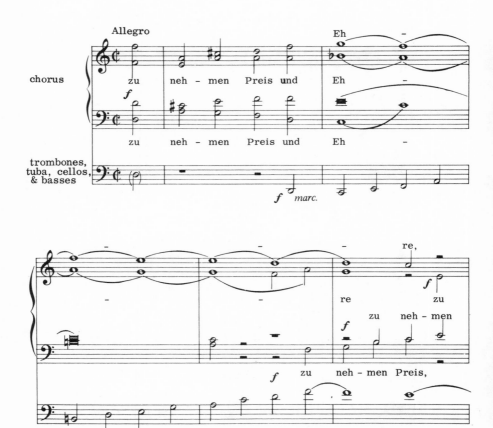

"DIE ERLÖSETEN DES HERRN"

After these *tours-de-force*, Brahms returned to the more informal, allusive style of the earlier examples. The next chamber work, the FIRST STRING QUARTET, uses many of the techniques that were exploited to imposing architectural purpose in the *Deutsches Requiem*, but naturally enough imparts to them the conversational flavour associated with chamber music.

Later still, works like the PIANO TRIO NO. 3 in C Minor (1886) and the CLARINET TRIO (1891) conceal polyphonic touches of no less ingenuity beneath an even more casual surface.

PIANO TRIO NO. 3

PIANO TRIO NO. 3

CLARINET TRIO

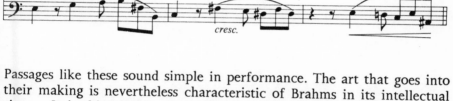

Passages like these sound simple in performance. The art that goes into their making is nevertheless characteristic of Brahms in its intellectual rigour. It is this combination of easy grace with unflagging logic that sets his polyphony above antiquarianism, just as it gives validity to the processes of formal organisation to be discussed in the next chapter.

4: Symphonic Thought

If there is one area in the complex craft of composition where Brahms has generally been accorded something like the credit due to his mastery, it is his handling of large-scale form. Sonata movements and other large structures make up the bulk of his official output, and also of the even greater number of works eventually excluded from it by his reluctance to approve for publication anything but a small proportion of the pieces he actually completed. In working on them he developed a sheer dexterity in the marshalling of musical materials that has had to be acknowledged by hostile critics as well as by admirers.

A notable exception, admittedly, was Bernard Shaw, who in his early days as music critic of "The World" habitually dismissed Brahms as a miniaturist *manqué*. "Strip off the euphuism from these symphonies," he inveighed in 1890, "and you will find a string of incomplete dance and ballad tunes, following one another with no more organic coherence than the succession of passing images reflected in a shop window in Piccadilly during any twenty minutes in the day. That is why Brahms is so enjoyable when he merely tries to be pleasant or naïvely sentimental, and so insufferably tedious when he tries to be profound." But Shaw was a special case. Towards the end of his long life he apologised for missing the point of Brahms's idiom. It was a failure natural enough in one whose principal critical hobby-horse, as far as the music of his own youthful years was concerned, was the championing of Wagner, and in this context it is suggestive that in 1876, before he had identified himself with the Wagnerian cause, he had described the G minor Piano Quartet—ironically enough, one of Brahms's least compactly organised works—as "a sufficient example of the genius of a master of whom we in this country know far too little."

Few critics, and by implication few members of the eager audiences that make an all-Brahms concert one of the safest one-man shows an impresario can mount, have felt inclined to echo the waspishness Shaw directed at Brahms during his years as the Compleat Wagnerite. It is nevertheless true that a species of historical accident has coloured much even of the more enthusiastic thinking and writing about Brahms, and in particular about his treatment of form. Because of the estrangement that grew up between Brahms's partisans and the Liszt-Wagner camp after the cordial enough amenities of Brahms's visit to Weimar in 1853, too little attention has been paid to the central importance of thematic transformation as a Brahmsian formal resource.

Tovey was one of the few commentators to have been fully aware of this importance. He was careful at the same time to emphasise that the logic of thematic connections, in any music, cannot avail to build genuinely organic form if the deeper logic that depends in sonata style on the handling of tonality is wanting. But though this is a valid caveat, the device of thematic transformation still offers the best point of entry for a listener looking to understand Brahms's formal methods, since it is in his use of it, and in his unprecedented elaboration of other closely related techniques of motivic development, that his greatest and most characteristic contribution to the history of musical form lies.

Composed in 1853, before the diplomatic break that was to obscure the purely musical issues, the PIANO SONATA NO. 3 in F minor abounds in transformations too obviously Lisztian to be missed even by partisans in the Nineteenth century's own belated *guerre des bouffons*. The opening bar of the first movement is subjected to a gradual process of modification that strongly recalls Liszt's own Piano Sonata, which Brahms had heard the composer play in Weimar a few months earlier.

(*see overleaf*)

Yet the Liszt influence is not the end of the story behind these Brahmsian exercises in thematic alchemy. Liszt is no more the originator of such devices than Brahms. The true ancestor of both these sonatas is a work

Allegro maestoso

whose influence on Nineteenth-century musical thinking has scarcely been recognised—Schubert's "Wanderer" Fantasy, which is really the first symphonic poem, and without which Liszt's essays in that *genre* could hardly have been conceived.

The nub of the method borrowed by both Liszt and Brahms can be seen not only in the way Schubert bases all four sections of the work (whose beginnings are shown as *a, b, c,* and *d* in the example) on the same idea, but also in his evolution of other themes from this basic material (as in *e, f,* and *g*). The affinity is clearest in the last three fragments of the Brahms example, which evolve step by step from the basic figure in exactly the same manner as the subsidiary themes in *f* and *g* of the Schubert.

In his maturer works Brahms moved away from such step-wise processes and turned instead to a subtle method of transformation that produced a world of difference in an instantaneous stroke. It was Tovey, again, who pointed out the distinction between such instantaneous Brahmsian transformations as that of the main theme in the development section of the first movement of the PIANO QUINTET

and the exhaustively gradual methods Beethoven used in transforming material like the opening theme of the "Archduke" Trio. When Beethoven, for his part, makes an instantaneous change in the atmosphere of a theme, he tends not to transform the entire rhythmic shape of the original in Brahms's manner but rather to modify only the melodic surface. This is what happens in the first movement of his Fourth Symphony

where a transition figure from the exposition is turned by embellishment into a graceful cantilena in the development section. The underlying thematic identity of the two passages is carefully maintained, which makes it all the odder that commentators have failed to notice the connection—the cantilena version is often cited as an instance of Beethoven's daring in introducing completely new material at a late stage in the progress of a movement.

Only occasionally does Brahms emulate Beethoven's way of altering the musical perspective by remodelling only the surface of a theme. An instance is the simplification—almost an anti-development— of the main theme in the last movement of the FIRST SEXTET.

More often in Brahms the elements are given an entirely new musical shape, as in the first movement of the same work, where the second of the three main themes gives rise to a fresh melodic creation with touching lyrical effect.

Liszt himself would probably have enjoyed a stroke of that kind, as he would have enjoyed, in the FIRST SYMPHONY, the new shape given at the coda to the main theme of the Finale.

Falling somewhat between the foregoing extremes of easy recognis-ability and cunning concealment is an instance in the FOURTH SYMPHONY that Alan Walker has pointed out in "A Study in Musical Analysis." At its climax, the third movement precisely foreshadows the theme of the Finale,

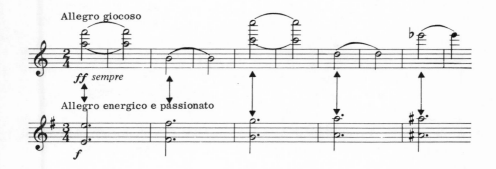

and yet the atmosphere of the two passages is so different that it may take several hearings for the listener to be aware of the link.

I shall return a little later to the First and Fourth Symphonies to take a more detailed look at the extraordinary richness of motivic interplay that marks both works. On the broader level of thematic transformation, the last example suggests another area of symphonic thinking in which the results have varied—depending on the skill of the composer—from profound illumination to banality: the use of characteristic themes, or motto themes as they are often called, to link the movements of a multi-movement composition. Here at least there is for Brahms, instead of the emarrassing parallel of Liszt, a good friendly precedent in Schumann's use of the technique, though once again Schubert's "Wanderer" Fantasy stands as an earlier source common to both.

All multi-movement works of real symphonic calibre depend for their coherence on unities of thought that span their entire form, whether these unities lie in the realm of dynamic key relations expounded by Tovey or in niceties of motivic organisation of the kind explored by analysts from Schenker and Schönberg to Hans Keller and Alan Walker. The large-scale correspondences of theme now in question are merely a special case in the genus of motivic development. They constitute a resource particularly easy for composers to misuse, because the slightest deficiency of taste or judgement will suffice to obliterate the line between the lucid and the banal. An unsuccessful attempt at motivic inter-relation on a small scale will simply escape the listener's notice, whereas a clumsy piece of broad thematic derivation will hit him between the ears. But here, as in other spheres, Brahms subtilises all he touches. In the THIRD SYMPHONY (1883) the transformation of the heroic opening theme at the end of the Finale,

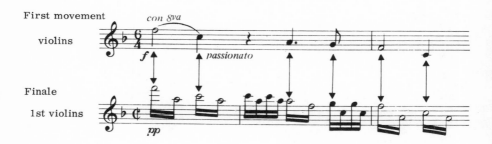

while clearly perceptible at first hearing, has the character of magical allusion rather than prosaic cross-reference; and even the more literal re-use of second-movement material in the Finale of the same work is poles removed from the mechanical crudity of similar devices in Franck's Symphony and Tchaikovsky's Fifth.

Particularly delicately disguised, not only through its complete change of emotional character but by shift of accent and difference of articulation, is the way the main Finale theme of the HORN TRIO is foreshadowed near the end of the preceding slow movement

and it is worth noting, too, a case like the Scherzo of the PIANO TRIO NO. I in B major (1854), where—this time within the span of a single movement—the glowing B major theme of the Trio section is just as shadowily prefigured in the main body of the Scherzo.

SCHERZO :

TRIO :

Running right through Brahms's output is a still more specialised device for building organic form which may be called thematic extension. The composer takes a detail that has first appeared either in isolation or in a wider thematic context at one stage of a work, and uses it later on as a springboard for the creation of an entirely new melodic shape. This method, which was to be developed a generation later into a central organising principle by Sibelius, is used imaginatively by Brahms very early in his career—the FIRST SERENADE exploits the idea with a piquancy that suggests the verbal device of the pun. In the first movement, the initial figure of the main theme is expanded in the development section into a naively square eight-bar theme of quite new character

which is then further expanded in its turn, and in the succeeding Scherzo the second bar of the opening theme, transferred to the dominant key, grows with the utmost naturalness into a lyrical subordinate melody that sounds equally new.

In the Finale of the FIRST SEXTET, it is a figure first heard near the beginning of the movement in an essentially accompanying role that provides the springboard.

This time the growth into a new shape is a two-stage process, in which a contrapuntal development of the original statement

acts as half-way house just before the lyrical expansion of the reshaped theme.

In maturer works like the FIRST SYMPHONY the method is used, as might be expected, with a still more ingenious touch. The sustained violin melody in the development section of the first movement sounds like a new theme, but it is a similar extension of a taut little figure heard much earlier.

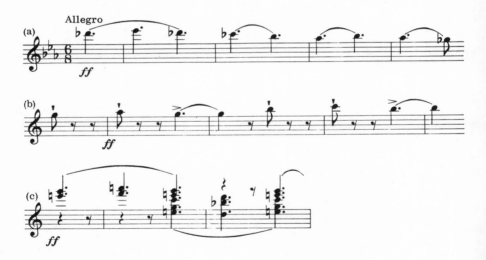

It is the difference in articulation between the sharp accents of the first version and the *legato* of the second that obscures the connection, which is nevertheless underlined a moment later—at *c* in the example —when the "new" shape is once again broken down to reveal its genesis.

This thematic grouping forms, moreover, part of a network of connections that spreads its influence through three of the four movements. The figure *c* in the example above is recalled a full half-hour later, just before the end of the symphony, in the exultant octave-unison of violins, violas, and cellos.

But as the adjacent-note figure x takes wing and expands, the shape it develops in the second half of the example can be traced back through a series of transformations as far as the slow movement.

Examples *a*, *b*, and *c* show respectively the appearance of the phrase in the exposition of the Finale, its syncopated precursor in the introduction to the movement, and its ultimate origin near the beginning of the Andante Sostenuto. Yet even this is not the full measure of Brahms's organising power, for the figure x is also clearly related to the two-note progression A–G in the main theme of the movement (see example on page 89) and to the F–G–F of the chorale figure taken from the introduction and presented in full orchestral splendour a moment before the octave-unison figure near the end of the Symphony already quoted.

What started by looking like a simple piece of thematic extension can now be seen to have led inexorably towards the crucial Brahmsian technique of motivic development, and one further illustration from the FOURTH SYMPHONY may serve as a natural quasi-symphonic transition to that subject.

Here a tiny descending triplet figure in parallel thirds, shown in *a*, is expanded almost at once into a smooth, spacious melody, and the texture is enriched at the same time by the figure of falling melodic thirds (indicated by the notes marked *x* in the example) that is nothing less than the thematic germ of the entire symphony.

It is a short step from this example to the general topic of motivic unity and Brahms's handling of it. Motivic development is thematic transformation writ small, the composer being concerned now with small groups of notes, or even with single intervals, rather than with extended themes. The falling thirds of the last example are a classic instance of the way Brahms derives the largest musical organisms from the smallest of thematic cells, and it will later be seen in the chapter on The Musical Flavour that such falling thirds provide a kind of stylistic fingerprint identifying and linking his most diverse works.

At the start of the Fourth Symphony the melodic line in the violins consists of seven successive falling thirds—two of them are converted by octave transposition into rising sixths, but the characteristic downward sweep is not obscured—and this statement is then answered by a series of six rising thirds.

1 : An autographed photo-portrait of the composer

2 : Some of the last pictures

Ein deutfches Requiem: Erfter Choreinfatz

3: Ein deutsches Requiem. *Above: the first choral entry*
Selig sind die da Leid tragen, *in the autograph. Below: an*
exhilarating example of Brahmsian counterpoint from the
fugue Der Gerechten Seelen sind in Gottes Hand *(see p. 78)*
(Breitkopf & Härtel, Leipzig/Ernst Eulenburg Ltd.)

4 : *The tenement building in Hamburg's dockland quarter where Brahms was born in 1833*

5 :*View of the Karlskirche from the apartment at Karlsgasse 4, Vienna, where Brahms lived from 1872 until his death in 1897 (Breitkopf & Härtel, Leipzig)*

Schönberg was apparently the first observer to point out the expansion of this basic idea at the twenty-ninth variation of the passacaglia Finale, where the series is stretched to eleven falling thirds with only a single octave transposition in the middle.

Yet the influence of this one figure is more pervasive still. Fairly obviously, the nervous syncopated whisper of the above example is at once echoed in assertive canon by the next variation. But the falling-third *motif* can also be traced in the accompaniment to the passionate B minor subordinate theme in the first movement, through the *sotto voce* woodwind figure in the development section, to the *legato* transitional phrase played twice by the woodwinds in the third movement and the cadential phrases of the fourth and seventh variations in the Finale (for the latter see *x* in the example on page 35).

Moreover, the melodic influence also spills over into the harmonic language of the work, as much in the rich successions of thirds and sixths in the slow movement as in the outer movements.

The very opening of the symphony illustrates this tendency to thicken the line harmonically in thirds, as the woodwinds hesitantly echo the main theme,

and the passage points at the same time to another characteristic of Brahms's musical thinking: his concern for organic integrity of texture. More than any other composer, at least of the Nineteenth century, he suffuses the textural lines of his music with essential thematic material. Often he uses a figure from one section to accompany new thematic material in another, as in the G MINOR PIANO QUARTET, or takes a mere transitional tag and makes it serve as accompaniment, as at two places in the FIRST SERENADE.

FIRST SERENADE

It is this gift for textures in which hardly a note could be spared without damage to the argument that most sharply differentiates Brahms from his *protégé* and admirer Dvořák: the surface of Dvořák's music often carries the imprint of Brahms's influence, but what goes on beneath it lacks the latter's organic unifying touch.

The opening bars of the FIRST SYMPHONY are especially noteworthy in this context. Fiercely single-minded in its drive for unity, the work begins with a superimposition of two thematic lines, one climbing in arduous chromatic steps, the other similarly descending, and from these two figures practically everything in the first movement, and much beyond it, is derived.

In the Finale, again, the unifying phrase is presented at the very outset, and from it are derived not only most of the main thematic developments, but also the *ostinato* accompaniment to the gracious subordinate theme, so that not even the most "relaxed" sections of the movement are excluded from the rigorous pursuit of symphonic unity.

But it is perhaps the SECOND SYMPHONY that is the most prodigious of all Brahms's works in the wealth of material it extracts from the three-note figure of its first bar. The example below illustrates its workings with a number of brief quotations taken from all four movements, and a few minutes with the score will suffice to show that this seemingly formidable array of cross-references is merely a selection taken from hundreds of instances.

FIRST MOVEMENT

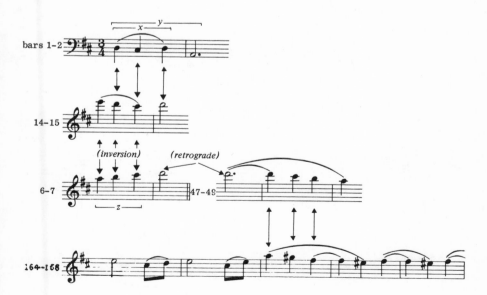

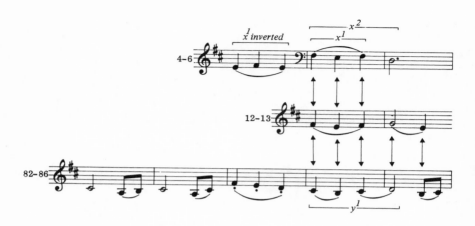

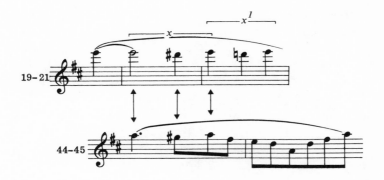

SECOND MOVEMENT

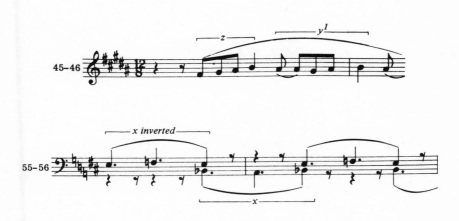

THIRD MOVEMENT

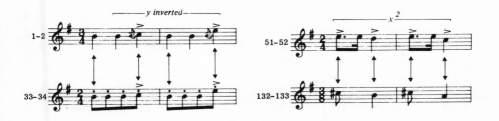

FOURTH MOVEMENT

*

    The reader who generally listens to his music without recourse to scores or illustrated programme notes may suspect that, in thrusting these intricacies before him, I am putting too much weight on technical detail. Brahms, he will argue, was probably not even conscious of the more abstruse among these thematic derivations—why, then, should the listener try to keep up with them all? It is true that intuition plays a large part in any real composer's formal thinking. For that very reason, intuitive unities offer the ear no less valid ground for understanding than those consciously planned by the composer. To seek by study to make them explicit is not in any way to diminish their point in underpinning the structure of a masterpiece, but it does add at least the innocent pleasure of seeing "how it works," and at best the heightened satisfaction of a developed insight into musical essentials. The questions "why?" and "how?" can continue to enrich experience as long as one does not lose the sense of wonder that prompts their asking.

    Understanding can also enhance pleasure in Brahms's fartherranging moments of tonal originality. The end of the development section in the first movement of the FIRST SYMPHONY will grind fearsomely on the listener's ear whether or not he understands why: the

*

B minor into which the music plunges is far removed, in the scheme of classical key relations, from the C minor towards which the course of the movement seems to have been hurtling. He may even, if he knows a little about sonata forms, consciously expect C minor as the traditional key for the start of the recapitulation. But it is only when one realises that B minor here gains much of its effect by reflecting the eerie *pianissimo* shift into an equally unexpected B major at the start of the development section that Brahms's daring stroke makes sense as well as drama.

Basil Lam once observed that the bold dislocations of expectation for which Carl Philipp Emanuel Bach was celebrated often amount to no more than "the too easy paradoxes of a style in which anything may happen." It is only in the framework of an established body of musical practice that strokes of originality can have a meaning beyond that of mere eccentricity. Against such a background Brahms is never afraid to use tonality in unorthodox ways, but, as the episode in the First Symphony illustrates, there is always a rational new principle to justify the variance from convention: it will not be left hanging in the air as an isolated, inexplicable phenomenon to challenge astonishment rather than satisfy a sense of logic.

Another case—occurring, like the one in the First Symphony, at the start of a recapitulation—is the unexpected substitution of an E major for a B flat major chord in the first movement of the FIRST PIANO

CONCERTO. Tovey calls this "one of the grandest surprises in music since Beethoven." This time the justification is a forward-looking one, prefiguring the ingenious rearrangement of keys later in the recapitulation, and in particular the poignant use of E minor in the course of a long modulating passage for the orchestra.

When expressive balance and formal cohesion demand it, Brahms is equally willing to effect a massive reshaping in the internal structure of a sonata movement. The first movement of the G MINOR PIANO QUARTET launches into its recapitulation, not only in G *major*, but with the subordinate instead of the main theme. The tonal and thematic circle is completed later, and there is more than a hint of the "arch" form—essentially, ABBA—adopted in this century by Bartók and Berg for many of their works.

More characteristic of Brahms is the notion of shifting the balance of a sonata movement by postponing development until after the recapitulation of the main theme. The device is especially useful to him in finales. By the time a large-scale work has reached its last movement, the listener's powers of concentration have already been taxed by a broad range of musical argument, so that a rather faster mode of action is called for. This can be achieved by hastening the return of the principal subject, and the need for working out the material may still be satisfied later when the movement is felt to be more firmly on its course. Brahms begins to experiment with this kind of foreshortening in the A major Piano Quartet and the Piano Quintet, but its fullest expression is found in the Finale of the First Symphony.

What all these instances show is that Brahms's symphonic thought, like his rhythmic method, is an equilibrium of freedom and strict formal principles. In viewing him as a crabbed classicist, a number of commentators have failed to perceive the freedom, a failure the more ironic in that Brahms's devoted general audience has evidently never been subject to it. To complain, as one writer has done, that the first movement of the Second Piano Concerto "too noticeably parallels that of Beethoven's Emperor Concerto" is to be diverted from understanding profound originality by purely superficial resemblances. The marshalling of solo-tutti relations in the two movements may reveal obvious similarities, but a critic who would understand Brahms must look beyond these to the crucial difference of thematic function in Brahms's first big piano solo, and further still to his radical modification of classical ways with key in a concerto ritornello.

Where modern composers, rather than critics, are concerned, Brahms's influence as a symphonic thinker has been more consistently beneficial than I have argued is the case with his rhythmic innovations. Even when the abandonment of classical tonal tensions—and thus of the dynamic basis of sonata form—rules out the possibility of stimulating contrast between foreground procedures and background expectations that enriches and diversifies his music, the procedures themselves remain valid. Contemporary composers vary enormously in their ability to develop really vital forms and to generate contrasts of scale and movement, partly because of the undermining of pulse discussed earlier. But the example of Brahms has helped almost all of them in the quest for formal unity.

5: Brahms the Colourist

To judge from many writers about Brahms, including even some of the more admiring ones, the very title of this chapter embodies a contradiction. Whatever qualities are ascribed to his music, a broad and enterprising range of tone-colour is not generally among them.

Like most misjudgements about Brahms, this one has little to do with the actual aural experience of his music. It derives rather from two more or less extraneous considerations. One is the fact that on several occasions Brahms changed his mind about the best instrumental vehicle for a particular musical inspiration, and that in some cases he published a work in two or more versions. The First Serenade, described in its final version as "for full orchestra," started life as a nonet for flute, two clarinets, horn, bassoon, and string quartet. The Piano Quintet passed through previous incarnations as a string quintet and a sonata for two pianos before reaching the form in which we know it best, and Brahms actually published the two-piano version as opus 34b, just as he was later to publish the Horn Trio in a version for viola and the *St. Antoni Variations* in both its original two-piano and its orchestral form. He made violin and viola versions of the two late clarinet sonatas. And the most complicated case concerns the curiously interwoven origins of the First Piano Concerto (whose first movement was originally intended as part of a symphony), the *Deutsches Requiem* (whose second movement, the ghostly 3/4 funeral march *Denn alles Fleisch es ist wie Gras*, began as the slow movement of the same symphony), and the First Symphony (which reuses, more than twenty years later, other material first conceived at the same period).

The facts are clear. Yet to draw from them, as some have done, the inference that Brahms knew little and cared less about instrumental colour seems to me about as sensible as to suggest that Schubert, because he cheerfully transposed his songs to a variety of pitches for different singers, was insensitive to the sound of voice and piano—or, for that matter, that Beethoven's radical re-shapings of material through long successions of sketches show him to have been a poor and irresolute practitioner of musical form-building. Much more relevant is the originality and obvious concern for colour effect demonstrated by the omission of violins throughout the Second Serenade (1859, revised 1875), and by their absence again from the first movement of the *Deutsches Requiem*, where the consequent tonal warmth is heightened by the division of violas and cellos into two and three parts respectively.

In any case, the proper evidence for Brahms's gifts as a tone-painter must be the actual sound of the finished music, not the preliminary history of a series of works, and the same holds true for the other red herring that has misled some listeners: the warping of judgement that results from intoxication with the spectacular orchestral effects of such composers as Liszt, Wagner, Rimsky-Korsakov, Mahler, and Richard Strauss. If in the light (or dazzle) of their very different approach Brahms's orchestration seems, by comparison, scarcely noticeable, the point is a fairly superficial one, and not at all to his discredit. For, as Stravinsky observed, "It is not, generally, a good sign when the first thing we remark about a work is its instrumentation, and the composers we remark it of—Berlioz, Rimsky-Korsakov, Ravel—are not the best composers." Readers may variously dispute the inclusion of Berlioz, or Ravel, in the roll of dishonour, or may even mischievously wonder whether the *Firebird* ballet qualifies Stravinsky himself for a place, but the general argument can hardly be denied.

It would be a mistake, moreover, to suppose that the colour qualities of music depend entirely on the handling of specific instruments or voices. A composer's way with harmony and texture can be just as much a determining factor as individual *timbres* for the colour of his work. In Brahms, the doubling of melodic lines in parallel thirds, in sixths, or in complete chords is (as will be illustrated further in the chapter on The Musical Flavour) the most common harmonic texture of all, and it has an unmistakable influence on the tone quality of his music, contributing alike to its depth and mystery, to its richness, and to its cutting edge.

A tiny figure from the slow movement of the FIRST SEXTET

is enough to show how doubling a line in thirds can add a touch of almost impersonal mystery, avoiding the more outward-looking expressiveness that a single violin, or two violins in unison, would have had at this juncture. A passage from the slow movement of the DOUBLE CONCERTO (1887) demonstrates the purely enriching, "luxury" effect obtainable from parallel thirds and sixths,

enhanced in this instance by the characteristic tang of the clarinets in the middle of the texture. The fifth of the ST. ANTONI VARIATIONS offers a striking illustration of the incisiveness of thirds;

the doubling of the woodwind lines here adds a "ping" to the attack rather like that contributed by the harpsichord continuo in the music of more than a century earlier. Something of the same crispness, with a touch of romantic warmth too, can be felt in the imitative embellishment of the main theme by flutes, clarinets, and bassoons at the beginning of the FOURTH SYMPHONY.

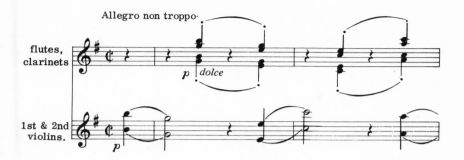

It is worth remembering that the wind instruments had begun to play an expanding part in orchestral music during the latter half of the Eighteenth century, partly as replacements for the earlier continuo; it is possible to imagine a particularly inventive harpsichordist adding just such embellishments to the texture of a baroque concerto or sonata.

Another typically Brahmsian use of texture as a colouring agent is to be found in his fondness for bare octaves. Four horns in three octaves (the middle one is doubled) introduce a sudden chill of mystery soon after the beginning of the ACADEMIC FESTIVAL OVERTURE (1880).

This impressively hollow effect is used with particular power when the octaves emerge from a piece with a fairly rich general texture, like the song FELDEINSAMKEIT (1878) where they are attached to the image of death, or the B flat minor INTERMEZZO for piano (1892); the octave passages shown overleaf are the only such bars in the two pieces concerned.

FELDEINSAMKEIT

INTERMEZZO

In the *poco allegretto* third movement of the THIRD SYMPHONY the spreading of the main theme, at its last appearance, over divided first violins in octaves, with cellos another octave below, produces a sudden gleam of brightness—at once expressive and cold—among the predominantly warm, dark colours of the movement.*

But beyond all such instances of purely textural colour, there is abundance enough of telling instrumental effects in Brahms for listeners whom the technicolour of the professional orchestrators has not yet blinded to the more solid tones of a real composer. Perhaps the most striking range of effects comes from the new independence often given to woodwind instruments and horns in his orchestral textures. A number of Brahms movements actually begin with winds playing either alone or discreetly supported by the lower strings, the violins entering only later—an effect rare in his forerunners' music.

The opening of the *St. Antoni Variations* is a special case, for the form in which the theme is first presented takes over directly the oboes, bassoons, contrabassoon, and horns of its Eighteenth-century original. But Brahms never did anything mechanically: the manuscript shows that he at first intended to score the statement of the theme for strings. (Another little-known change of mind transformed the beginning of the Fourth Symphony, where the initial violin theme was originally to be prefaced by two bars of wind chords.†)

In several other movements the idea of an all-wind opening was kept. Of the symphonies, the Second allows cellos and basses to introduce and support sixteen bars otherwise given to horns and woodwinds, but the first and second movements of the THIRD SYMPHONY both begin with the sound of wind instruments undiluted.

---

* Conducting such orchestras as the Berlin Philharmonic and the Philharmonia—both in their best years—Furtwängler and Carlo Maria Giulini were able to impart a rare touch of poetry to this passage in their recordings.
† I once heard these two bars in a performance recorded by George Szell for a demonstration record, and very odd they sounded to an ear familiar with the opening in its usual form.

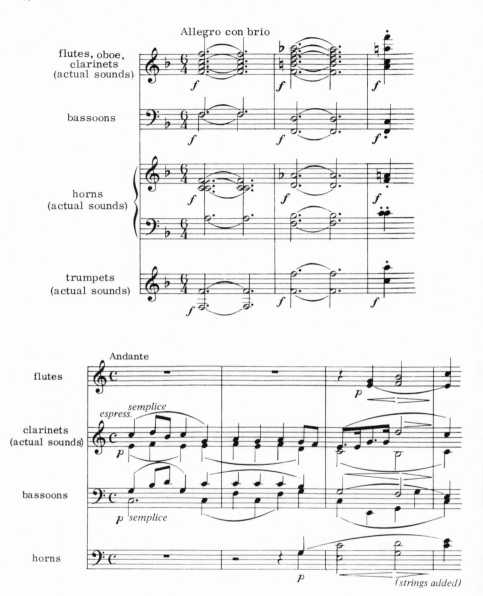

The first-movement example is essentially introductory, though the figure contained in the first flute, oboe, and horn parts is developed later in the movement, but the beginning of the Andante is fully thematic, as is the long wind-supported oboe solo, after two introductory bars on bassoons and horns, in the Adagio of the Violin Concerto.

Two other places like these are the slow movement of the Fourth Symphony, with a four-bar introduction of horn and woodwind figures based on the main theme, and that of the Double Concerto, where the opening horn-call and answering woodwind figure form an augmentation of the first four notes of the theme immediately following.

Beethoven is generally regarded as, *par excellence*, the "liberator" of the orchestral winds. Yet, though Mozart had already shown the way with the opening bars of his B flat major Piano Concerto, K450, this manner of beginning an orchestral movement appealed less to Beethoven—who only tried anything like it in the first movement of the Violin Concerto and the last two movements (the latter for a special, essentially extra-musical effect) of the Ninth Symphony—than to Brahms. Similarly, one has to go back to the occasional stretches of serenade-like wind writing in Haydn's symphonies, or the many in Mozart's symphonies and piano concertos, to find a precedent for such passages in the middle of movements in all Brahms's symphonies, in the *Deutsches Requiem* and *St. Antoni Variations*, and in the *Academic Festival Overture*.

BRAHMS : SECOND SYMPHONY

HAYDN : SYMPHONY NO. 92

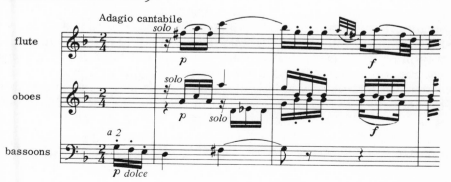

MOZART: SYMPHONY NO. 39

Apart from an occasional parallel like the bucolic three-horn Trio in Beethoven's "Eroica" Symphony and a few wind-band effects at light-hearted moments in Schubert's earlier symphonies, there is nothing like these examples in the three-quarters of a century between.

Brahms also had his favourite instruments. Again and again in his music, outstandingly eloquent passages for the horn, the clarinet, and the cello testify to the special attraction these instruments had for him. That is should be just these three—the warmest in tone of the brass instruments, the woodwinds, and the strings respectively—is itself significant: the predilection (like the omission, already mentioned, of violins in the Second Serenade and the first movement of the *Deutsches Requiem*) emphasises that richness, rather than brilliance, is the characteristic of Brahmsian sonority.

The most obvious evidence of Brahms's interest in horn, clarinet, and cello is his composition of a number of works specially for them: a trio for horn, violin, and piano; a trio, a quintet, and two sonatas featuring clarinet; and two cello sonatas, as well as the Double Concerto for violin and cello. There are, admittedly, three sonatas and an individual concerto for violin, but then the violin was much more of a "standard" solo instrument, and even Brahms's own instrument, the piano, is hardly favoured by him to the extent that his own need for concert and recital material might lead us to expect. The preference, however, goes far beyond these special works. It can be felt all through the web of his instrumental writing. His taste for the horn carries an additional qualification: unlike Schumann, he never accepted the valve horn, with its full chromatic scale, which was beginning to make its way into use during his early years, but remained faithful to the older natural horn. (He insisted that even the Horn Trio should be specifically designated for the natural instrument on its title page.) This meant that his horn parts had to be restricted to the notes of the natural overtone series, which has many gaps in its lower reaches, or otherwise filled out by the device of hand-stopping. But the restriction, like any restriction accepted by a creative artist, cannot be regarded in a purely negative light. Brahms felt that the greater purity of tone and intonation more than compensated for the smaller gamut of notes available. That this was his order of priorities cannot be unconnected with his taste for themes based on arpeggios of the common chord. Peter Latham, in his book on Brahms, devotes some space to suggesting that the frequent appearance of such themes is a weakness in the composer's style, but does not offer any very substantial grounds for his view; the reader may be forgiven for wondering quite *why* scale themes, or any other theoretical category of themes, should be regarded as somehow "better" than arpeggio themes. Brahms's taste seems to me closely connected with an unwavering concern that his music, whatever constituent factors went into its construction, should always *sound*, and it may well have contributed specifically to the unblemished euphony of his counterpoint, since chordal themes can usually be combined more naturally in a harmonic context than themes based on conjunct motion.

For the horn itself, smoothness of execution is another consequence of Brahms's attitude. Being planned within the technical confines permitted by the natural instrument, his horn parts not only are perfectly practicable without valves but, *a fortiori*, fall more readily beneath the player's fingers and lips when the valved instrument is used than comparably ambitious parts in other composers' music. The unmistakable "horn-quality" of his themes for the instrument is particularly well illustrated in the Finale of the FIRST SERENADE, where a subsidiary theme first played by the violins evokes the character of the horn so vividly as to make its later restatement by that instrument seem absolutely inevitable (the example below gives the horn version, but the melodic shape of the original violin statement is identical).

1st horn
(actual sounds)

p dolce e espressivo

On the horn, this exhilarating tune sounds not so much to be travelling instrumentally as to have come home.* The fourth movement of the *Deutsches Requiem*, the fourth of the *St. Antoni Variations* (a duet with oboe that foreshadows the poignant style of the solo in the third

---

* With respect to sheer practicability, it is pertinent to observe that, in the Brusilow/Chamber Symphony of Philadelphia recording of the Serenade, this entire movement and the preceding Scherzo, which also contains an abundance of solo horn work, were recorded in a single take—without any need for subsequent "repairs" of detail—at the end of a long session. However much credit was due to the horn player, some must redound also to the composer for his understanding of the instrument.

movement of the Third Symphony), and the lead-back to the recapitulation in the first movement of the Third Symphony are a few among Brahms's many other superb characterisations of the instrument.

The luxuriant solo, extending to twenty-four bars, in the coda of the Second Symphony's first movement is perhaps the most famous of all—this work as a whole is as happy a hunting-ground for a principal hornist as Mahler's Ninth—but the shorter solo at the start of the SECOND PIANO CONCERTO is, set beside the superficially similar opening of Schubert's "Great C major" Symphony, even more revealing of Brahms's love for the sheer sound of the instrument.

BRAHMS

SCHUBERT

Schubert, by scoring his opening for two horns in unison, deliberately plays down the individual quality of the sound in favour of the strongly architectural character of this introduction; Brahms's use of a single instrument places all the emphasis on the intensely personal poetry of unsupported horn tone, and this is borne out by the continued association of the theme with the instrument later on at two of the most magical moments in the movement.

Home environment may well have been an initial factor precipitating Brahms's intimate understanding of the horn, since he must often, as a child, have heard his father playing and practising the instrument. With the clarinet, the specific stimulus that led him, between 1891 and 1894, to devote his last four chamber works to a relatively unusual solo instrument came from the playing of Richard Mühlfeld, clarinettist in the ducal orchestra at Meiningen. The four works thus stem from a special relationship rather like that of Mozart with Anton Stadler, who likewise inspired the composition of Mozart's great works for the instrument. But in Brahms's case the clear predilection for the clarinet goes back much further: it might, indeed, be fair to say that his entire orchestral output assigns to it the leading

role among the woodwind choir played in Mozart—no less characteristically—by the oboe. As early as the Eighteen-Fifties, the original
nonet version of the First Serenade included one flute, one bassoon,
and two clarinets, but no oboe, and the clarinets kept the musical
limelight when the work was rescored for orchestra. (By contrast, it
was only in a later revision that Mozart allotted to clarinets many of the
fine passages given to the oboes in the first version of the G minor
Symphony, K550.)

Brahms particularly liked to resort to the gentleness and warmth
of a single clarinet, played quietly in the middle register, at the ends
of slow movements. This use of the instrument in the SECOND SYMPHONY
(and a similar passage in the fifth movement of the *Deutsches Requiem*)
evokes Mendelssohn's clarinet scoring, and was later to be echoed by
Mahler in the second *Nachtmusik* of his Seventh Symphony.

BRAHMS

MAHLER

The solo clarinet also plays a primary thematic role in the third
movement of the First Symphony. The characteristic sonority of the
subordinate theme in the first movement of the THIRD SYMPHONY and
of the slow movement theme in the FOURTH is the sound of clarinets—in
the first case a solo instrument, in the second a pair playing mostly in

luminous thirds.

THIRD SYMPHONY

FOURTH SYMPHONY

The slow movements of both works depend heavily on clarinet tone, and in the Andante of the SECOND PIANO CONCERTO the two clarinets are elevated to the status of virtual chamber-music partners with the piano in six long-breathed bars that amount practically, apart from the discreet support of the orchestral cellos, to a trio.

This same movement is the *locus classicus* for Brahms's orchestral use of the cello: the principal cellist is given the responsibility of stating the main theme as a long solo, in an orchestral texture that also divides his *tutti* colleagues into two parts. Cellists may regret that Brahms did not leave them a solo concerto—he said when he saw the score of Dvořák's Cello Concerto late in life that he would have written one himself if he had realised the capacity of the instrument—but they have something to console them here and in the Double Concerto.

Massed orchestral cellos also have some fine moments in Brahms, and the instrument is never neglected in his chamber music, whether in trios, quartets, and quintets, or in the still richer textures of a movement like the *andante, ma moderato* variations of the First Sextet.* Beyond the strictly thematic context, Brahms's use of the cello in accompaniment shows a rare grasp of its character: at the restatement of the subordinate theme in the first movement of the C MINOR PIANO

---

* The first cello part in the Sextet naturally tends to sound even more than usually sonorous and eloquent when it is played by someone like Casals, but the Casals Festival recording nevertheless offers an object-lesson in giving due prominence to the instrument without distorting the musical balance at the expense of the upper lines.

TRIO, Tovey singled out the cello part of the *pizzicato* string accompaniment for comment, remarking that "there is not one composer in a hundred, especially among 'great colourists,' who could be trusted not to make chords of them instead of single notes."

He went on to explain that "the bass of such chords vanishes before the top, unless the player puts all his accent below, a precaution which is impossible in any tone above mezzo-forte," and thus that "single notes, which look so humble on paper, provide the only sonorous bass, and . . . give all their weight to the chords of the violin."

*

The effects considered so far in this chapter are all essentially "normal." But as well as developing the use of instruments along what might be called standard lines, Brahms is perfectly capable of enjoying himself in the special-effects department. The only thing that keeps the doubters unconvinced is that he rarely seeks effects of the more obvious kind—the injection of an irreverent triangle into the otherwise irreproachably sober textures of the Fourth Symphony, and the use of the same instrument in the *Academic Festival Overture* (where it joins cymbals and bass drum in the biggest orchestra he ever employed), remain exceptions in his work.

Much more Brahmsian in its subtlety (and therefore easier to miss) is the extraordinarily original use of the piccolo in the TRAGIC OVERTURE. Even comparatively experienced listeners are surprised when they discover that this usually obstreperous instrument has a place at all in what must rank as one of Brahms's most serious and unshowy works—for it appears in only 15 of the overture's 429 bars, and then exclusively in the untypical *pianissimo* of passages like the following.

The composer's way with the timpani is equally unobvious. He is readier than most of his predecessors, though less so than Berlioz, to use it unaccompanied or semi-solo, but of the five instances shown below

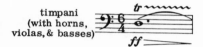

SECOND SYMPHONY

VIOLIN CONCERTO

FOURTH SYMPHONY

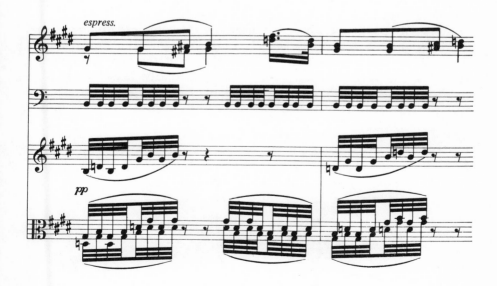

FOURTH SYMPHONY

only two are in the instrument's familiar dynamic mode—the other three are strikingly poetic and evocative of mystery.

Brass instruments, again, are used for purposes far different from the martial ones commonly associated with them. The low trumpets that unobtrusively punctuate the main theme of the First Symphony's Finale at the recapitulation produce a particularly magical patch of colour. Trombone and tuba, supported by *pianissimo* woodwinds and strings, are used with a wonderful tone of hushed suspense in the TRAGIC OVERTURE,

though this time the first movement of Schubert's "Great C major" Symphony provides a clear precedent.

Mystery is the most frequent aim of Brahms's instrumental explorations. It can be found in the similar effect of bare wind octaves against a hushed string background, this time *tremolando*, in the SECOND PIANO CONCERTO;

in the scurrying muted strings, again heightened by bare octaves, in the Scherzo of the C minor Piano Trio; in the muted strings, marching in massed parallel chords, of the second movement of the *Deutsches Requiem*, and the muted violin of the Scherzo in the G minor Piano Quartet; and in the eerie violin harmonics of the Finale of the Fourth Symphony.

In the use of voices, Brahms's imagination is most strikingly shown by a passage from the fourth movement of the *Deutsches Requiem*, where the basses, by repeating a phrase just sung by the tenors at the same pitch, achieve a complete contrast of tone by the simplest means. But a purely instrumental touch in one of his last works, the CLARINET TRIO,

will provide the most appropriate conclusion for a chapter that argues Brahms's stature as an original colourist, for in this imperceptible transfer of the line from clarinet to cello (the moment of interchange almost impossible for the ear to pinpoint) one can see the germ of the *Klangfarbenmelodie* ("tone-colour melody") technique for which Schönberg and Webern were later to gain such a reputation as pioneers.

6: Lyric Melody:
Brahms's Attitude to Words

In a composing career stretching over four decades and a half, Brahms produced more than 200 solo songs with piano, 25 vocal duets, 27 quartets in addition to the *Liebeslieder* and *Neue Liebeslieder* waltz sequences, 14 accompanied choral works, a dozen sets of unaccompanied choral pieces, 20 vocal canons, and more than 100 folksong arrangements for solo voice or chorus. The solo songs alone span the distance from his third published opus to his last but one.

The list embodies a substantial proportion of Brahms's entire output, and so it will not be surprising if his approach to the problematical art of word-setting provides some insight into his style as a whole. Brahms himself saw nothing inappropriate in linking purely instrumental music with verbal associations: he even added the words of the folk-song *Verstohlen geht der Mond auf* under the melody in the slow movement of his first published work, the C major Piano Sonata. Forty-one years later, in 1894, writing to Clara Schumann about the set of *Deutsche Volkslieder* he published in that year, he pointed out that early allusion to what is also the last song in the set, remarking that the connection "ought to represent the snake that bites its own tail

—that is to say, to express symbolically that the tale is told, the circle closed." But, he went on, "I know what good resolutions are, and I only think of them and don't say them aloud to myself": fortunately for us, the impulse to compose a few more works, including the great *Vier ernste Gesänge*, overruled his "sensible" intentions.

In the opening song, *Liebestreu*, of the very first set Brahms published there is, within the first four lines of the setting of Reinick's text, a clue to the source of Brahms's characteristic rhythmic variety.

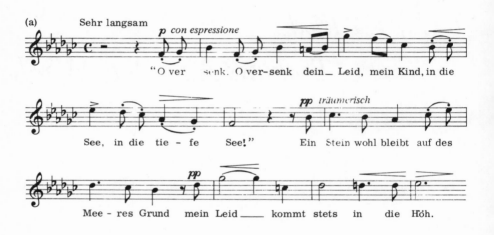

(a) Sehr langsam — *p con espressione*

"O ver senk. O ver-senk dein_ Leid, mein Kind, in die See, in die tie - fe See!" Ein Stein wohl bleibt auf des Mee - res Grund mein Leid____ kommt stets in die Höh.

(b)·

mein Leid kommt stets in die Hoh.

b in the example shows what might have been the obvious way to set the fourth line. The more regular phrasing is perfectly natural in its relation to the poetic rhythm: it is also rather dull. By placing the emphasis of his response on the crucial word *Leid* ("grief") and stretching this expressive syllable out to three full crochets, Brahms expands the square background phrase-length of four bars to five and brings air and life into what would otherwise have been merely a smooth and agreeable little ditty.

The central place of this expressive device in Brahms's vocal idiom can be seen in dozens of instances from the early *Mondnacht* (published

6 : *The Castle at Detmold where Brahms spent three autumns (1857–59) in charge of the court's music. Above : a contemporary lithograph by A. Noltsch. Below : the castle today (Bibliographisches Institut, Leipzig/Detmold Tourist Board)*

7 : *Brahms at the piano. Above : a contemporary drawing of him accompanying his close friend, the singer Alice Barbi, in the Bösendorfer-Saal, the principal Viennese hall of the period for song recitals and chamber music. Below : a caricature by Willy von Beckerath (L. Bösendorfer Klavierfabrik)*

8 : The young Brahms (seated) with Joachim

9: *A photo-montage of Brahms at his work-desk. The original photograph showed only the room, and the composer's image was superimposed later*

without opus number in 1872 but probably written in 1854) to *Ständchen*, op. 106 no. 1, and beyond,

MONDNACHT

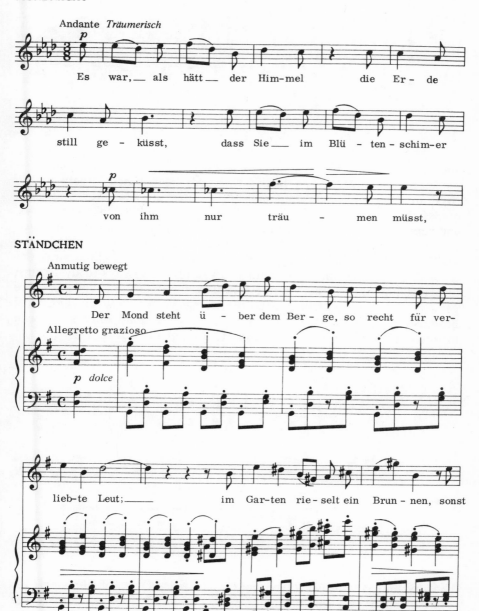

Stil - le weit _____ und breit.

and it may well be that the experience he gained, as a sensitive reader of poetry, in doing justice to words contributed largely to the rhythmic freedom and suppleness of his instrumental works. This is one of those matters, admittedly, where it is possible to take two views, and some have held rather that it was instrumental style that dominated Brahms's approach to song writing: he was, writes Eric Sams in his BBC Music Guide to the songs, "above all a musician, seeking an outlet through poetry for his own feeling. His songs are always ready to turn into instrumental music." But I find Tovey's opposite diagnosis more persuasive when he claims that "the theme of the slow movement of Brahms's A major Quartet shows rhythms that could only have been invented by masters of the musical treatment of words."

The rhythmic feature involved here is not irregularity of phrasing over a broad span but, on a smaller scale, Brahms's fondness for triplet rhythms and his propensity for combining threes with twos. The natural progression from word-inspired freedom of rhythm to instrumental freedom can be seen more clearly by comparing two other songs from opus 3, *Liebe und Frühling I* and *Lied*, with phrases in the slow-movement themes of the SECOND and THIRD STRING QUARTETS.*

LIEBE UND FRÜHLING I
(Revised version)

LIED, OP. 3 NO. 4

---

* Even beyond such particularities of rhythmic structure, it can be argued that Brahms's instrumental writing in general—and especially, as might be expected, his use of the solo violin—has strong links with certain aspects of vocal style. Thus there is more than a hint of the traditional methods of *bel canto* in the suppleness of phrasing that gives Kreisler's and Krebbers's recordings of the Violin Concerto their profoundly persuasive character: the affinity is to be found in the way both violinists fill each bar to its utmost limits with music, much in the manner of a singer like Julius Patzak in his prime. His superb recording of Donizetti's *Una furtiva lagrima* is a good instance. This elasticity of line is, again, closely allied to the more general qualities of Brahmsian rhythm discussed earlier, for it similarly achieves freedom without undermining the pervasive influence of rhythmic pulse.

SECOND STRING QUARTET

THIRD STRING QUARTET

The move from twos into threes does not occur only at cadences but extends to every segment of Brahms's vocal lines. A typical passage like the middle of the powerfully lyrical song *In Waldeseinsamkeit* shows how readily it leads to the superimposition of threes and twos that is the fingerprint of Brahmsian texture (see opposite); and the degree of freedom that can ultimately result from such methods may be observed in *Beim Abschied*, op. 95 no. 3, which carries the technique to its logical conclusion.

IN WALDESEINSAMKEIT

(Schoss) und mei-ne be-ben-den Hän-de um dei-ne Knie ich schloss,

BEIM ABSCHIED

müh mich ab und kanns nicht ver-schmer-

Other composers before and since Brahms have shared his ability to capture the inner meaning of a poetic text, and one at least —Schubert—surpasses him in this regard. Much rarer, and for that very reason the source of a good deal of unjust and uncomprehending criticism of his song style, is Brahms's unwillingness to be diverted from the central poetic and musical vision for the sake of surface illustration or irrelevant symbolism. Since long before Bach, composers had been in the habit of seizing happily on every sort of occasion for word-painting. The voice would go emphatically down when it met the word "grave" and up at the first glimpse of "heaven," and these are only the two most obvious of hundreds of examples. The effect of these devices is to add to the listener's musical experience a certain innocent pleasure through recognition of the correspondence of sound and sense. But such an effect can never be an adequate substitute for the more substantial musical virtues—for strength and proportion of line or for coherence of harmonic progression. Taken in isolation from these essential elements, verbal illustration is, quite literally, valueless, by which I mean neither good nor bad. Brahms as a composer for the voice is content to use the device when it does not conflict with his broader purpose. There is, certainly, a special aptness, in the earlier example from *Ständchen*, both in the lengthening of note-values and in the *pianissimo* of the accompaniment at the words *Stille* and *weit*, and these touches work together with the more general expansion of the phrase and, as it were, decorate its surface. But where a more literal-minded composer would have felt the need to continue the treatment on *breit* ("broad"), for which it would be at least as appropriate, Brahms, having at this point achieved exactly the scale of phrase he is seeking, refuses to be deflected a moment longer and resumes the basic pulse of the song without further delay.*

For Brahms, the technique of song lies ultimately in creating a lyrical image for the idea of the words, and then letting it do its work by purely musical logic instead of allowing it to change direction at the dictate of every new verbal twist. This is perhaps the truth rather too effectively concealed in Sams's "instrumental music" remark. Once again, the underlying integrity of pulse is central to the issue, not any

---

* The listener's perception of such points as these depends to a great extent on performance. Of the three singers whose versions of the song are included in the list of recommended recordings, Fischer-Dieskau captures Brahms's fine distinctions with the utmost clarity, and Hotter is very nearly as precise. On the other hand, Schlusnus pulls the tempo about so drastically and prolongs the syllable *breit* so much that the subtleties are obliterated. His record is, indeed, included among the recommendations purely for the sake of its vocalisation: there is a certain sensual pleasure to be had from hearing Brahms songs projected by one of the finest baritone voices of the century, even while it is clear that the singer's gifts are better suited to the broader, more operatic style of, say, some of Richard Strauss' songs.

specifically instrumental quality in Brahms's thinking. The flexibility of his phrasing, in song as in any other medium, makes its effect precisely because there is a background regularity for it to bite against. In this respect, Schönberg's views about "musical prose" (see the chapter on Brahms as Rhythmic Inventor) are singularly inapposite to Brahms's songs, for his approach to the different claims of expressive cohesion and rhythmic continuity on the one hand, and of textual pointing on the other, is essentially the poetry rather than the prose aproach. It is this that aligns him with Schubert and strongly opposes him to Wolf.

Much of the more carping criticism that has been levelled at Brahms's word-setting stems from erecting verbal illustration into a spurious principle (instead of a purely ancillary technique) and then applying it to the composer least, of all great song-writers, interested in the technique. Peter Latham's comments on one of Brahms's finest songs—*Von ewiger Liebe*—exemplify the fallacy. Picking out the point where the established 6/8 metre in the voice part is fused with a change to 3/4 in the piano, and somewhat reluctantly acquitting the composer of deliberate cynicism, he nevertheless describes is as unfortunate "that he chooses the precise moment when the girl proclaims 'Our love shall last for ever' to put voice and piano out of step."

(*see overleaf*)

It is certainly possible to imagine a setting of Wenzig's poem that would bring previously diversified rhythms and textures into a new climactic unity at the crucial words. As a piece of innocent symbolism, the effect would be agreeable enough. But that is not the only way to penetrate the meaning of a poem, and it is not Brahms's way. To denigrate a magnificent piece of climax-building along such lines is to let abstract ideas about music, and specific (and superficial) criteria drawn from an entirely different style of word-setting, take the place of intelligent response to what Brahms is actually trying to do. Max Harrison, who in his book "The Lieder of Brahms" sees clearly that "the influence of the singing voice is apparent in all but the sternest moments of Brahms's symphonies," allows himself to be sidetracked into similar irrelevancies when he complains of the lack of "authenticity" in Brahms's songs on texts with foreign, and specifically oriental, associations. The notion that there is a "required idiom" (Harrison's phrase) for such settings might be appropriate in evaluating a musicological dissertation; it has nothing to do with the work of a composer concerned to draw on his sources purely in the degree to which they serve his own creative purpose.

Other misconceptions arise from an altogether too foursquare

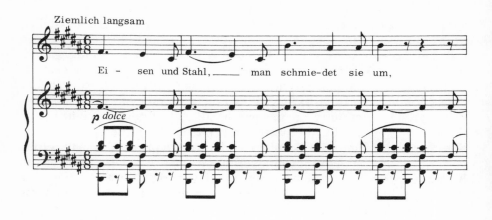

Ziemlich langsam

Ei - sen und Stahl, _____ man schmie-det sie um,

un - se - re Lie - be, wer wan - delt sie um?

un poco animato e cresc.

Ei - sen und Stahl, sie kön - nen zer - gehn,

un poco animato e cresc.

un – se – re Lei – be, un – se – re Lei – be muss

e – wig, e – wig be – stehn!"

ritard. molto

approach to the analysis of rhythmic structure. Latham, again, complains about poor declamation in *Die Mainacht*, finding unwanted accents on the words *wann, durch,* and *und.*

The argument ignores the intimate link of continuity that binds *durch* and *und,* across the underlying beat structure, to the words that precede them, and it also fails to take account, where the first word, *wann,* is concerned, of the all-important qualifying factor of pitch—if Brahms, instead of what he actually wrote, had offered us some such unnatural formulation as shown below, then there might have been something to complain about.

Schubert himself, whom no composer of German Lieder surpasses in sensitivity to words, begins *Gute Nacht,* the first song in *Die Winterreise,* by putting the relatively unimportant word *bin* on the main beat of the bar.

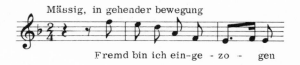

But as in *Die Mainacht,* the beat pattern cannot be considered in isolation from the relative pitches of the words: the placing of *fremd,*

on the last quaver of the previous bar, just a semitone above *bin* master-fully reconciles the sense and feeling of the words with the underlying regularity of the iambic verse-metre.

The truth is that Brahms and Schubert alike—in common, as Tovey saw, with Dowland two centuries earlier—are working with a conception of rhythm far too subtle and too supple to be defined within the terms of a single musical element such as metre. Harmonic movement, melodic shape, and syllabic colouration enter into it too, and if one fails to take them into account one inevitably misses the point of any great vocal writing. A useful parallel, though an incomplete one, can perhaps be found in Vergil's handling of Latin hexameters. In a line like

|Īnfán|dūm, rē|gínă, iŭ|bēs rĕnŏ|vārĕ dŏ|lórem|

the conflicting accents (in normal speech) of the words *infandum* and *iubes* and the rhythms of the metric structure pull against each other; not until the last two words is the conflict resolved, in a similarly satisfying blend of movement and repose.*

There is one general exception to Brahms's usual disinclination to allot a specific, ultimately symbolic coloration to individual words, and that is in his response to the idea of death. The hollow octave passage in *Feldeinsamkeit*, quoted in the previous chapter, is one instance, and it also illustrates his frequent association of the idea with the musical image of falling melodic thirds. The association comes to its most moving expression in the third of the *Vier ernste Gesänge* (*Four Serious Songs*).

(a)

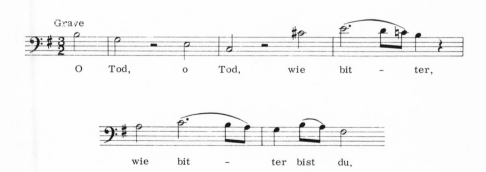

---

* "Aeneid," II, 3. The verse rhythms are shown by the diacritics — (long) and ᵕ (short), the stress accents by ʹ.

(b)

O   Tod,   o   Tod, wie   wohl_____ tust du,

a shows the beginning of the song, and *b* the transformation of the bare falling thirds into rising sixths as the image of death's bitterness is succeeded by that of its benevolence. The beginning, too, of the first of the *Vier ernste Gesänge* illustrates the continuity of response evoked from Brahms by the thought of death, for it clearly recalls, after a space of thirty-eight years, the opening of the austere *Begräbnisgesang* (*Funeral Hymn*) for chorus, wind instruments, and timpani, composed in 1858.*

VIER ERNSTE GESÄNGE

Andante

p
Denn— es— ge - het dem Men - schen wie dem Vieh,

BEGRÄBNISGESANG

Tempo di marcia funebre

p

basses & bas-
soon in unison

Nun— lasst uns— den   Leib— be - gra - ben,

Ultimately, except in passages like this, it is probably the broader working of Brahms's musical mind that strikes the listener first, where in Schubert it is the immediacy of the poetic response. For that reason, Brahms's songs are unlikely ever to rival Schubert's in wide popularity.

---

* The *Begräbnisgesang* is one of those Brahms works scarcely ever heard in the concert hall. But it is a compact, moving piece, and Zdeněk Mácal has recorded an excellent performance of it.

But in recognising that, we need not do Brahms the injustice of under-estimating him by listening to his music through ears cluttered with the symbolism of Wagner or the exhaustive verbal allusiveness of Wolf.

7: The Musical Flavour

In the preceding chapters we have looked at a varied array of methods and expressive modes that seem to be, in one sense or another, Brahmsian. But there is no valid purpose in taking a composer's work apart unless we also try to put it together again: to understand the whole it may be necessary first to understand the parts, but it is still necessary to understand the whole. Among the multiplicity of traits we have examined, what is it that makes Brahms sound like Brahms?

Perhaps the most constant thread running through the argument has been that connected with various musical manifestations of the number three: harmonic thirds in the chapter on colour, falling melodic thirds in the context of symphonic thought and the setting of words, triplet figures and combinations of threes with twos especially in the field of rhythmic invention. Without making a numerological fetish of this association of ideas (for Brahms was not one of those composers fascinated by numerology), it is fair to say that these elements together provide the basis for much of his language. Just as firm rhythms, scale-wise motion in melody, and the typically dynamic fifth (the dominant-tonic relation) in harmonic movement are central to Beethoven's style, so the flowing triplet and the lyrical third are the fundamental ideas in Brahms. Their deployment covers all the dimensions of his musical space: the harmonic third is a vertical formation, the triplet rhythm is horizontal, and in their different ways the melodic third and the superimposition of triplets and duplets project themselves in both dimensions at once.

I have already shown how Brahms uses parallel thirds to achieve a particular colour effect. But the use of thirds and sixths in their harmonic context determines the sound of his music also in a more far-reaching way: it gives it its characteristic weight and texture. Instrument for instrument, the sound of Brahms is heavier and thicker than the sound of most other music. The full-throated, full-hearted sound of the start of the slow movement in the FIRST SERENADE derives its gravity (in both senses of the word) not only from the low register of the instruments—though that is a factor—but also from the harmonic flavour of the thirds, and their packed sonority likewise tempers the texture of the woodwind passage later in the movement.

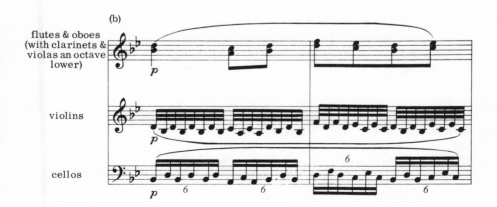

The second and last movements of the *Deutsches Requiem*, the graceful, dotted-rhythm woodwind theme near the beginning of the third movement of the First Symphony, the antiphonal exchanges of woodwind and strings in the Finale of the Second Piano Concerto, the piano countersubject of the variations in the slow movement of the C MAJOR TRIO,

and much of the Andante of the Double Concerto all take their character from the saturation of their harmony with thirds.

Brahms's predilection for thirds shows itself too in the key-relations of the inner movements of his cyclic (multi-movement) works. In Haydn, Mozart, and Beethoven, slow movements in particular tend (though there are many exceptions) to be pitched either a fifth above or a fifth below the home tonics of major-key works—that is to say, in either the dominant or the subdominant key, with some preference for the subdominant since it is the more "reposeful" key in relation to the tonic. Brahms is not only much readier than his predecessors to risk a completely monotonic key scheme: of thirty-seven cyclic works, no fewer than six (the First and Third Piano Trios, the First Piano Concerto, the Horn Trio, the Second String Quartet, and the Second Clarinet Sonata) have all their movements founded on the same keynote. He also clearly rejects the preoccupation with relations of fifths in favour of third-related keys. Of the twenty-four slow movements not set in the home tonics of their parent works, sixteen are in either the mediant or the submediant, and only seven in the dominant or the subdominant. (The odd movement out is the Adagio Affettuoso of the Second Cello Sonata, whose flat supertonic relation has already been discussed and traced to its historical precedents.)

In the rhythmic sphere, the fluid, liberating effect of triplets is audible at once even when they appear free of the complexity of cross-rhythm. Nothing could be farther removed from squareness and stiffness than the gently rocking first bar of the A MAJOR PIANO QUARTET.*

But as the example shows, Brahms immediately creates a contrast by juxtaposing twos with the triplets in alternate bars. He cannot long resist the temptation to pass from simple alternation to simultaneity of threes and twos, and so arrives at the horizontal-vertical nexus that is at the rhythmic heart of all but a very few of his movements.

Other composers had combined threes with twos before Brahms. The example below illustrates two movements that have a strong family likeness—the slow movements of Mozart's C major Piano Concerto, K467, and of Beethoven's Fifth Piano Concerto.

MOZART

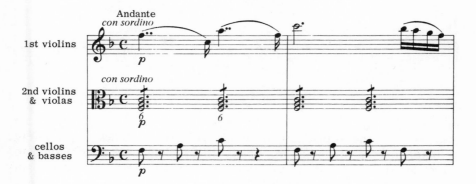

---

* The pianist's ability to relax—to let this initial phrase expand in its own time—is crucial to the atmosphere of the entire movement, which is why the otherwise good performance by George Szolchany with members of the Hungarian Quartet cannot match the charm of the Babin/Goldberg/Primrose/Graudan recording or of Rudolf Serkin's 1932 performance with members of the Busch Quartet.

But until Brahms seized on the device it was usually limited, as in those instances, to the supporting of duplet-rhythm melodies with purely accompanimental formulas in triplets. In Bruckner it was promoted to a broader rhythm-building function, but even here it tended to remain the by-product of an essentially melodic contrast. Only with Brahms —whose subtlety in any case far surpassed Bruckner's—did it become a fundamental element in the planning of rhythm, texture, and form alike.

I have already discussed the form-building process in action in the First and Second String Quartets (see Brahms as Rhythmic Inventor).

Texturally, too, both works are enlivened in every one of their movements by the triplet-duplet superimposition. The FIRST SYMPHONY is
another work where it can be found in all four movements—only
once (bar 340) in the first movement, but pervasively in the slow movement and Finale, and used to notable constructive purpose in the third
movement, where it binds the return of the 2/4 main subject firmly to
the 6/8 of the Trio section just before.

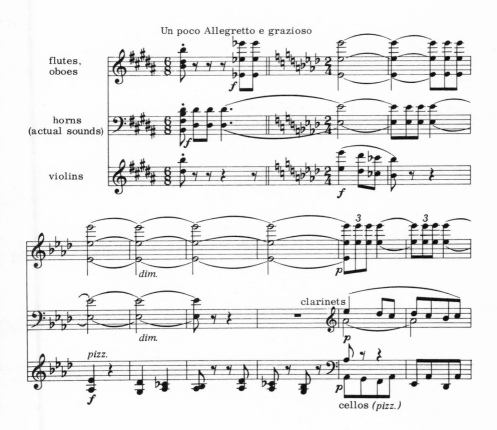

Brahms's other favourite rhythmic pattern is the dotted crotchet/
quaver or dotted quaver/semiquaver unit, which he often uses over
long stretches and as the basis of important themes. Again, there is
ample precedent for dotted-rhythm themes, and yet it is curious that,
since the time of Purcell and the later Baroque composers, the resource
had fallen into relative neglect. Thus, by comparison with his contemporaries and his classical predecessors, there is something quintessentially Brahmsian in the sound of such long chains of dotted figures

(often accentuated by the insertion of a rest) as in the TRAGIC OVERTURE.

violins

Looked at from the melodic instead of the rhythmic point-of-view, the passage also exemplifies one of Brahms's favourite linear shapes: an oscillating phrase that sometimes moves regularly between two pair of notes (as in the slow movement of the FIRST SERENADE), sometimes keeps one note constant while varying the other one (as in the SECOND SYMPHONY and the SECOND PIANO CONCERTO), and occasionally combines both kinds of motion in quick succession (as in the Finale of the THIRD STRING QUARTET).

FIRST
SERENADE

SECOND SYMPHONY

SECOND PIANO CONCERTO

THIRD STRING QUARTET

But characteristic as these note-alternations are, it is the falling-third figure (which we have already looked at in a structural context in the Fourth Symphony and in an expressive one in the song *O Tod, wie bitter bist du*) that most abundantly permeates Brahms's melodic writing. In varying degrees of prominence, and with a wide range of emotional connotations, more or less extended chains of falling minor and major thirds inflect the melodic line and sometimes the bass of at least twenty songs and more than a dozen major instrumental works.

In a relatively short three-step sequence, the figure generates the broad *andante* theme in the C MINOR PIANO QUARTET, and it returns, fragmentarily at first but then extending itself to no fewer than fourteen steps (including some rising sixths), in the Finale.

A five-step sequence, accompanied by a variant of itself embellished by rising thirds, provides the melody in the Andante of the F minor Piano Sonata (another sonata movement furnished with a poetic text, though this time purely as a superscription), and in the song ABENDREGEN the figure is broken down into fragments, distributed through the texture, and simultaneously doubled in thirds with a tautly-charged expressive effect. Other extended sequences occur in the Finale of the First String Quintet and in the first movements of the First String Quartet and the CLARINET TRIO. All three of these moreover embody dotted rhythms, and the instance in the Clarinet Trio (which also concludes with one of the oscillating figures considered above) is further expanded in the Finale first into a fairly complex sequence of thirty steps and then into a drastically simplified series of fifteen.

ABENDREGEN

CLARINET TRIO

*

It is time now to look from another angle at the various elements so far surveyed—the broader areas of musical thought covered in earlier chapters as well as the features of idiom summarised in this one—and see how they add up over the span of some complete works. The three I have chosen for the purpose are the First Piano Concerto, the Third Symphony, and the Clarinet Quintet. The point of these particular examples is to show how far the characteristics I have enumerated determine Brahms's style even in those works least frequently cited elsewhere in this book, and thus to emphasise *a fortiori* how deeply his entire output is imbued with these stylistic traits.

An examination of the earliest of the three works, the FIRST PIANO CONCERTO, completed in 1858, will serve moreover to suggest how trenchant an understanding Brahms had already reached in his early twenties of principles of the classical concerto style that the thirty-year-old Beethoven was just beginning to master in his Third Piano Concerto. There is a common notion that a symphony is somehow more respectable than a concerto, and the idea probably derives from the equally false belief that concertos are concerned primarily with technical display. The truth is that the concerto is in essence a dramatic form. It evolved from the canzone and other forms of earlier polyphonic music, it has strong links with vocal music (and particularly with the aria), and its point lies in the possibilities opened up by the affectingly human opposition of the individual to the mass. The exercise of instrumental virtuosity is certainly one of the ways a soloist can establish his dominance over an orchestral mass that could obviously, in terms of sheer noise-making ability, overwhelm him with ease. But far more important means are those qualities of poetry, sentiment, and wit —characteristically individual qualities—that give a good concerto performance its special fascination.

The crux of the classical form—as distinct from the simpler type of concerto pioneered by Mendelssohn—lies in its method of organising an initial orchestral ritornello and a succeeding solo (and orchestral) exposition to give scope to these qualities. The composer's two basic tools here are the distribution of themes and—no less vital in any style related to sonata—the handling of key contrast. It is in the latter sphere that the First Piano Concerto shows Brahms grasping at once what Beethoven, in his first two published concertos, had not yet realised: the necessity for the ritornello to maintain a degree of monotony (in the fundamental descriptive sense of the word) in order to heighten, when it comes, the solo exposition's effect of tonal diversity and freedom.

The principle remains equally valid (as the fully mature Beethoven of the last two piano concertos and the later Brahms of the Second Piano Concerto and the Double Concerto demonstrate) when the soloist is allotted a prefatory role to play even before the orchestral ritornello. With or without such a device, what matters is that the orchestra should not dissipate expectancy by indulging in too much movement and development itself. Brahms's special achievement, in the widened harmonic horizons of the mid-Nineteenth century, was to allow the orchestra a measure of tonal exploration without for a moment impairing the ritornello's sense of preliminariness.

In the First Piano Concerto the long-range planning that makes sense of the wrenching E major chord in the recapitulation (described in the chapter on Symphonic Thought) has its counterpart at the very start. The B flat major chord from which the orchestra launches the first theme similarly points forward to the one "foreign" tonal area of the ritornello—the B flat minor of the subsidiary theme first heard on violins, clarinets, and bassoons.

This mystery-laden figure is actually the second half of a transitional thematic complex that begins a few bars earlier with an equally shadowy and hesitant phrase in the home D minor,

and the two thematic elements between them provide the mainspring for much symphonic development as the movement proceeds. One favourite Brahmsian device—ensuring structural continuity by associating different melodic subjects with the same bass—is heard at the exultant D major codetta theme proclaimed by the full orchestra just before the end of the ritornello (compare the bass in this example with that in the last example above, and compare it, for that matter, also with the main theme of the movement).

Two other characteristic methods of thematic development—transformation and extension—are used when the paired themes recur in the development section. Here the second half is first telescoped in diminution into what sounds like a new theme, and then extended into yet another one in combination with a *pizzicato* viola figure (x in the example below) which is itself a foreshortened transformation of the movement's opening theme.

For Brahms, even the degree of unity secured in the codetta theme by referring back to an earlier bass is not enough. Between top line and bass, the violas and first bassoon provide a further thematic strand: a halfway house between another orchestral theme heard just before and the melody with which the piano introduces itself a moment later.

The effortless manner in which this magnificent solo subject establishes the piano's dominance exemplifies concerto thinking at its strongest. So does the tonal scheme of the movement as a whole, which—apart from the excursions to B flat minor and E minor—is grand, plain, and thoroughly classical. And so, again, does the piano's eventual introduction, in F major and at a slightly slower tempo, of the "real" second subject,

for, together with the soloist's very first entry, the second subject is
traditionally the juncture in a classical concerto movement at which
the solo instrument most decisively asserts its individuality.

But this second solo theme, like its predecessor, cunningly under-
pins concertante drama with symphonic logic. It is not merely derived
in part (as the figure *y* illustrates) from the earlier theme: it also points
directly forward to the main theme and first principal episode of the
Finale, shown respectively in *b* and *c* of the next example.

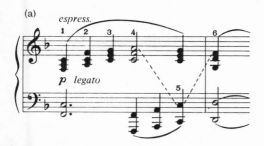

(c)

(d)

violins

Further symphonic ramifications are to be found throughout the Finale, and they reach their most concentrated form in the diminution effected in the last dozen bars (*d* in the example), where the major mode strengthens the sense of unity with the first-movement origin of the figure.

In addition to touches of Brahmsian colour like the prominent horn solos in the first and last movements, and to a version of the falling-third *motif* in the latter,

piano

the Concerto is rich in characteristic rhythmic ingenuities, such as the telling use of hemiola in the first two movements and the frequent superimposition of triplet and duplet rhythms in all three.

A typical resource is the ambiguity of the "shadowy and hesitant" transitional phrase already quoted from the first movement: the immediate restatement of this theme

1st violins, muted, & violas octave lower

lops off the first bar, thus reversing the rhythmic functions of the remaining bars and demonstrating in retrospect that the first bar of the initial statement was purely preliminary. In a subtle way this rhythmic idea too plays its part in the symphonic unification of the work, for the main theme of the slow movement

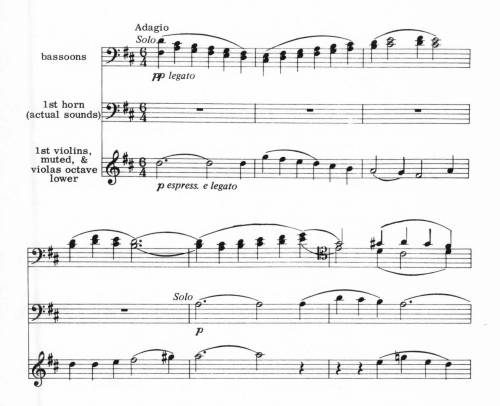

is also curiously ambiguous in its rhythmic placing, with a first bar that can likewise be regarded as falling outside the rhythmic structure of the theme.

But the stroke that is at once simplest and most quintessentially Brahmsian in its powerful rhythmic effect is to be found in the continuation of the piano's entrance theme in the first movement.

The unobtrusive addition of the quaver chord marked z in the second and fourth bars of the example brilliantly enhances the long-breathed quality of the passage by doubling the size of the phrase—imagine those bars without the extra notes, and the difference between talent and genius will be clear.

By the time the THIRD SYMPHONY was completed in 1883, another quarter-century of experience had taught Brahms how to compress an equally weighty argument within a shorter time-scale. Sheer economy and directness of expression are among the most immediately striking features of the work, and especially of its first three movements. The opening Allegro con Brio, for example, strides in only thirty-six bars to its subsidiary theme—a stage the First Symphony had taken nearly twice as many bars of compound time (plus a slow introduction) to reach. Such decisive motion gains time for the composer so that, when the Finale is reached, its relative expansiveness has all the more effect.

The symphony brims with instances of Brahms's personal taste in textural and instrumental colour, from the emancipation of the wind instruments in general exemplified by the openings of the first two movements and the frequent atmospheric use of octave doublings to the unusually prominent thematic role allotted throughout to clarinets, solo horn, and cellos. Typically, some of the finest effects derive their intensity from contrast with the economy that precedes and prepares for them: the sparing, and thus magical, use of high violins in the slow movement is an impressive case. Restraint of another kind appears in the unconventional use of soft dynamics to build a climax—witness the extraordinarily tense *pianissimo* in the middle of the third movement—and for that matter in the utterly untraditional recourse to *pianissimo* at the very end. Tchaikovsky's Sixth Symphony, Elgar's Second, and a number of instances in Mahler and Vaughan Williams have made the device of a quiet symphonic ending comparatively familiar to modern listeners. But to the audience at the first performance of Brahms's Third, very few if any of whom can have been acquainted with its only notable (and semi-programmatic) precedent in Haydn's "Farewell" Symphony, the effect of this bold renunciation of conclusive gesture must have seemed astonishingly original.

The falling-third *motif* appears fleetingly and unemphatically in the Andante but with considerable force both in the Finale (seven steps in the bass) and at the climax of the first movement (eight steps in the melodic line),

and another fingerprint of Brahmsian style is the long series of dotted figures that plays a prominent part in the exposition and recapitulation of the Finale.

In its quest for organic unity the Third Symphony draws as pervasively as all Brahms works on techniques of intricate motivic development, but much more emphatically than most on the device of explicit thematic cross-reference. The progress of the *motif* marked x in the following example is an excellent instance of motivic development from small components affecting wide musical spans. The figure can be clearly traced from its first occurrence in the main theme of the first movement, through a restatement with simultaneous inversion near the end of the Andante, to a further use in inverted form in the third movement theme, and the ends of the first and third movements (shown in *d* and *e*) underline the essential unity by drawing the contrasting moods of the initial statements closer together.

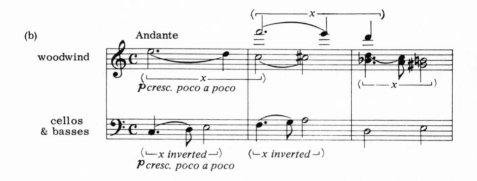

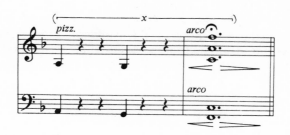

The same *motif* is alluded to at the very end of the symphony, by which point its identity has been well enough established not to be obscured by a change of rhythmic context.

The cross-reference between wider thematic units of which this allusion forms a part has already been cited in the chapter on Symphonic Thought, as has the other motto-style link between slow movement and Finale. But it is the three-note rising figure of the very first three bars, together with the A flat/A natural oscillation immediately following, that provides the symphony's most fundamental term of motivic cross-fertilisation. The note-sequence F-A-F had in any case a special significance for Brahms—it was, indeed, one of the very few expressions of extra-musical content in his vocabulary. As a young and romantically inclined musician, Joachim had adopted the phrase F-A-E —standing for *Frei aber einsam* ("Free but alone" or "lonely")—as his musical motto. Brahms had responded and picked up the challenge with a characteristic touch of stoicism by making F-A-F—*Frei aber froh* ("Free but joyful")—his own signature-tune.

The *motif* has already made its appearance in this chapter in the course of the D minor transition theme from the First Piano Concerto (where it is marked *w* in the example above). The next example demonstrates the much more far-reaching influence it exerts over three of the four movements of the Third Symphony—and *b* and *c* below, both taken from near the beginning of the Andante, show Brahms varying the allusion within the span of a single theme by first referring to Joachim's F-A-E formulation and then expanding the overall seventh to the octave of F-A-F to provide a fulfilling cadence.

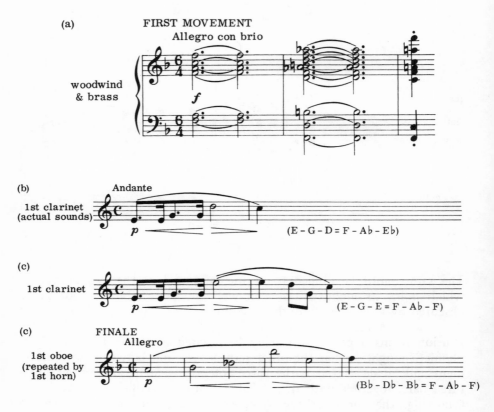

In its initial presentation by the wind instruments, the three-note rising figure may seem to be purely introductory. But within the next two bars a conflict between the original F-A flat-F form of the *motif* and the A natural of the symphony's official F major is set up, and this

basic minor-major opposition forms a crucial thread in the musical texture of the entire work. It is from this beginning that the choice of the minor mode for the main body of the Finale derives its logic. And the climax of this climactic Finale, and thus of the symphony as a whole, hammers the point home with a dramatic conversion of major into minor chord that connoisseurs of Mahler may acknowledge as foreshadowing the dialectical core of his Sixth Symphony.

BRAHMS

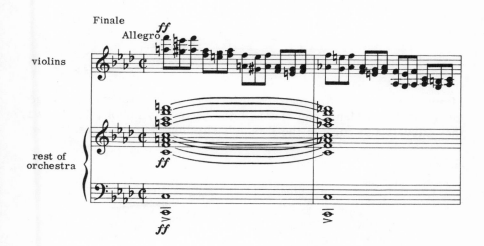

MAHLER

Rhythmically the work—especially in its first movement—is all fluidity and sinuous grace. Its peculiarly Brahmsian blend of flexibility and strength is exemplified in the opening out from 6/4 time to 9/4 for the subordinate theme (cited earlier, in the chapter on Colour) and in the subsequent further expansion of single 9/4 bars into two-bar phrases of 6/4 in the development section.

Meanwhile the basic 6/4 metre is also subjected to a variety of displacements no less violent than those of the Second Symphony in the way they subvert and confuse the listener's rhythmic expectations.

(c)

woodwind
in octaves

violins

In *c* particularly, the accent on the last crotchet of almost every bar easily overrides the regular 6/4 pattern, which has already been gradually obscured in the earlier parts of the example. Thus the ear finds it almost impossible not to shift its perception of the pulse forward by one crotchet—and the return to normality at the end of the passage administers a further jolt with the insertion of what by now sounds like an extra note. Moreover, the richness of rhythmic idiom dramatised in these "special effects" is conditioned also by a general background studded with hemiola and other cross-beat phrasings, with superimpositions of triplet and duplet rhythms, and—especially in the Andante—with the allusive use of triplets as a means of symphonic unification.

Composed eight years later, in 1891, the CLARINET QUINTET carries all these thematic and rhythmic techniques to the saturation point of Brahms's maturest style. The very first three bars of the work

provide starting-points for at least three distinguishable yet inter-related thematic networks that extend their combined influence over all four movements. The first and most obvious line of development is the motto-like return in both the second movement and the Finale to the characteristic outlines of this main theme.

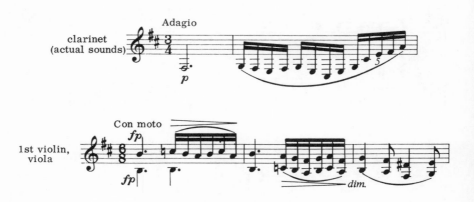

But then a tiny modification in the opening phrase, suggested at *a* in the next example, indicates the source of another group of themes, subtler but no less far-reaching in their interrelation. The gradual evolution of the figure is shown at *b* and *c* in two later formulations from the first movement and at *d* and *e* in its third-movement forms. The theme of the variation Finale, shown at *f*, tautly combines the outward melodic style of the third-movement theme with the actual notes (numbered in the example) of the second part of the work's opening theme, which has also been echoed at a different pitch in the third movement in the version seen at *g*.

The Adagio second movement is not omitted from this complex web of symphonic cross-reference. On a more minute level than the motto allusion already cited, the viola part in the accompaniment to the movement's main theme picks up a phrase last heard just a moment earlier near the end of the first movement, and itself derived from the chain of thematic links outlined in the last example.

Then the first three notes of the slow movement theme itself are used to underpin the movement's strongly contrasted central minor-key episode; and a last melodic twist, in the concluding moments of the Finale, reminds the listener of this theme in the midst of a section derived essentially from the first movement. This touch completes the binding together of all the work's thematic material.

In the matter of key relations the influence of the first few bars extends as comprehensively across the wider structure of the Quintet as in that of thematic organization. Melodically and harmonically, the beginning of the theme can be understood just as well in D major as in B minor. This ambiguity—far from conclusively resolved in favour of the home B minor in the course of the third and fourth bars—makes the observance of the exposition repeat more than usually important, because of the shift of meaning imposed on the clarinet's following D major arpeggio by its new context at the end of the section. The fundamental ambiguity is reflected, too, in the unconventional tonal treatment of the subsidiary theme, which makes its first appearance normally enough in D major (the movement's relative major), but then, in the recapitulation, eschews the "textbook" B minor or the slightly less traditional B major in favour of G major, as though it existed in a cloudless tonic-dominant world of major-key relations quite separate from the drooping minor inflections of the home key.

The pathos of this consummate touch of dramatic irony can only be heightened by the inevitable return to B minor. But the re-establishment of the tonic comes so close to the end of the movement that equilibrium demands the use of the same keynote for the second movement (though this time the mode is major rather than minor), and the sense of a pair of complementary tonal centres is again enhanced by the third movement's oscillation between the same poles of D major and B minor.

That unemphatic opening theme is productive, too, of a wealth of inventive rhythmic turns, beginning immediately after the clarinet's first entry in the fifth bar with a broad expansion of the initial one-bar phrases into two bars each, and continuing at the end of the movement with a reversal of the two main beats to produce a satisfyingly cadential feeling. This device is taken up when the theme returns in the Finale, and then in turn extended at the very end with still more conclusive effect.

Elsewhere the themes of the first movement are subjected to many ingenious touches of rhythmic displacement within and across the beat. But it is the theme of the Adagio that gives rise to the most arresting rhythmic inspirations of all. First, in anticipation of the 4/4 rhythmic structure of the episode, the basic three notes of the theme are extended to four—but within the established 3/4 metre.

At the end of the episode, the final bar of 4/4 is made to serve also as the first bar of the returning 3/4 theme—a classic instance of the pivotal or two-way phrase discussed in the chapter devoted to Brahms's Rhythmic Invention.

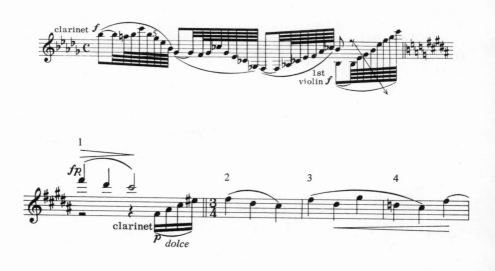

Of the Quintet's propensity towards specific instrumental tone-colours it is not necessary in this case to speak, since the unique character of the clarinet naturally informs the entire work. But it will be appropriate, for a last example, to point out the extremely effective reversal of instrumental roles early in the first movement at the point where, over sustained notes in the clarinet's lowest (*chalumeau*) register, the cello soars above the viola in a luxuriant texture founded mainly on parallel sixths and thirds.

It is pure Brahms, both in the originality of its sound, and in the way that originality is drawn from completely normal instrumental techniques combined in a fresh perspective.

*

The three works examined above in some detail combine with the many discussed and quoted earlier to round out the picture of a music remarkable rather for its warmth than for the brilliance of its colours. The textures are rich, not only because of Brahms's taste for harmonising in banks of thirds but because of the solidity and power of the bass line, yet the fluency of the polyphonic writing ensures transparency too. Most important of all, the atmosphere is an atmosphere of subtlety, of delicately poised ambiguities, in which the foreground structure is almost always backed by at least one other—and quite different—way of interpreting what may at first seem clear and uncomplicated.

Form, line, texture, and above all rhythm are characterised at once by freedom and by strictness: another ambiguity, or, rather, paradox. The vertical and horizontal dimensions of the music interpenetrate each other with an intimacy scarcely achieved in any music of the previous 250 years. A handful of the great composers before Brahms surpassed his mastery in one or another department of the art of composition, and a smaller handful were his equals or superiors in several spheres. It was his special gift to bring the various planes of musical invention into a closer unity than they had enjoyed since the Renaissance. It is in this, rather than in any woolly conception of musical prose, that his vital influence on the "music of the future" can be found.

The man that emerges from the music is a similar blend of contradictions and surprising juxtapositions. Brahms's emotions are as intense as any composer's of his time, yet he holds them usually in the tautest of reins. He is measured, averse to excess (witness his avoidance, after the early years, of extreme tempo indications, and his invention of a new kind of scherzo more moderate in speed and dynamic than Haydn's or Beethoven's), considerate, considering. He is generous, given to outbursts of lyrical feeling, impulsive. Yet he always explains his leaps of imagination, and never takes a risk or commits a breach of logic. He is never, like Beethoven, superhuman. That is not his way. Human he always is, and by turns exalted or gruff or gently playful or stoical, and just occasionally solemn enough to exasperate. And perhaps in all this, too, he is a composer for today. For our century, having seen what artistic and other varieties of totalitarianism can lead to has rather lost the taste for Titans.

Appendix

Selected Writings

Apart from the two-volume biography published by Brahms's English pupil Florence May in 1905 and republished in a new edition in 1948, the most accessible and useful books in English devoted to the composer are those by Geiringer, Latham, and Gál.

Karl Geiringer's "Brahms—His Life and Work" was published originally in German in 1934 and then in an English translation two years later. A second English edition, revised, enlarged, and provided with a new appendix of Brahms letters, followed in 1948 and had its fourth impression (George Allen & Unwin, London) in 1974. It is a most sympathetic study based on painstaking scholarship. On the other hand, Geiringer's comments on the music itself do not go very deep, but rather offer a blend of fairly colourful description with more or less conventional aesthetic judgement. The book is thus more valuable for its insight into Brahms's character and for its wealth of circumstantial detail about the works than for its music criticism.

Peter Latham's "Brahms," a Master Musicians series volume first published by Dent in London in 1948 and revised by Sir Jack Westrup for a new edition in 1975, is also, in its less ambitious way, better on the life than on the music. In earlier chapters I have offered some strictures about Latham's handling of purely musical points. But he is as warmly understanding of Brahms the man as he seems unsympathetic to his music, and his book constitutes a useful counterpoise to Geiringer's weightier treatment.

Hans Gál was co-editor with Eusebius Mandyczewski of the Vienna Philharmonic Society's collected edition of Brahms's works published by Breitkopf & Härtel in the Twenties. His "Johannes Brahms—His Work and Personality" is the most recent contribution to the general Brahms bibliography. Published originally in German in 1961, and in an American translation two years later by Knopf in New York and by Weidenfeld and Nicolson in London, it offers more than either of the books discussed above in the way of musical illumination.

Of the individual segments of Brahms's *oeuvre*, it is the songs that have lately received the most attention, with the publication in 1972 of Eric Sams's "Brahms Songs" (in the BBC Music Guides series) and of Max Harrison's "The Lieder of Brahms" (Cassell, London). Though, again, the reader of this book will have noted specific disagreements with parts of what Sams and Harrison have to say, both of their books provide helpful studies of an aspect of Brahms that has been too long neglected, Harrison at greater length, Sams with a crisper touch. Another BBC Music Guide, John Horton's 1969 study of the orchestral music, is descriptive criticism of the "how" rather than the "why" school : Horton reports what happens in the music without drawing any particularly perceptive conclusions about creative origins or effects.

It is to specific essays in books of wider scope that one must turn for what remains by far the most penetrating body of Brahms criticism —that of Sir Donald Tovey. This is contained in "Brahms's Chamber Music," published first in Cobbett's "Cyclopedic Survey of Chamber Music" (Oxford University Press, 1929), and then incorporated in Tovey's "Essays and Lectures on Music" (OUP, 1940); in individual essays (originally programme notes) on sixteen works (the *Deutsches Requiem*, the Alto Rhapsody, the *Schicksalslied*, and all the orchestral music), published by OUP between 1935 and 1939 in the six-volume "Essays in Musical Analysis"; and in the essays on the three piano quartets and the Handel and Paganini variations contained in the supplementary volume of "Essays in Musical Analysis" (OUP, 1944). Valuable, too, as much for its suggestive misunderstandings as for its many telling insights, is Schönberg's essay "Brahms the Progressive," most recently republished in 1975 in a new edition of "Style and Idea" by Faber in London and St. Martin's Press in New York.

Rather more application than is called for by Tovey's witty yet profound essays is needed by readers of Edwin Evans's four-volume "Historical, Descriptive and Analytical Account of the Entire Works of Johannes Brahms" (London, 1912ff) and of the standard large-scale biography, "Johannes Brahms" (also four volumes, Berlin, 1904–14), by the composer's friend Max Kalbeck. The latter work, moreover, is not available in English. Among foreign-language books, José Bruyr's much less ambitious "Brahms," published in Paris in 1965 by Editions du Seuil, is likely to be more attractive to the general reader. Its criticism—swashbuckling in the best French gnomic manner—matters less than the seventy-odd illustrations, which vividly evoke the atmosphere of Brahms's world.

The Music in Print

Brahms is luckier than some of his contemporaries and almost all of his predecessors in the quality of the published editions through which his work has been handed down. Eusebius Mandyczewski, who was keeper of the Vienna Philharmonic Society's archives during the last ten years of Brahms's residence in the city, represented a real link with the composer's own time when he co-edited with Hans Gál the twenty-six-volume Collected Edition published for the Society in 1926–27 by Breitkopf & Härtel in Leipzig. This edition, since revised and, in 1964, supplemented by the addition of the five songs for Ophelia written for a production of "Hamlet" in 1873 and unearthed by Mandyczewski's successor Karl Geiringer sixty years later, is the basis for most subsequent Brahms scholarship and publication.

For the concertgoer and record collector, the fifty-four-volume reprint of the Breitkopf edition published in New York in miniature format by Kalmus is in general the most useful source, and it is still relatively inexpensive. Especially helpful are such features as the inclusion of the original 1854 edition of the Piano Trio No. 1, op. 8, in one volume together with Brahms's 1891 revision, which is so drastic as to amount practically to a new work. Study of the two versions side by side is extraordinarily illuminating.

In the case of the songs, however, the equally inexpensive Lea Pocket Scores edition in eight volumes, also based on Breitkopf, is preferable, since it is furnished with better indices and with English translations of the texts, sensibly and undistractingly added at the end of each volume. Other miniature scores worthy of note are the extensive collection published by Eulenburg, most of which have the advantage of informative prefaces outlining the history of the work in question with copious quotations from Brahms's correspondence with publishers and friends, and the handful—limited, regrettably, to the four symphonies, the three string quartets, the *St. Antoni Variations*, and the *Gesang der Parzen*—in the Philharmonia series published by Universal Edition, which are the most clearly and attractively printed of all the Brahms miniature scores. Boosey & Hawkes and Heugel have also published a few Brahms works in similar format, but the Philharmonia (where it exists), Eulenburg, and Kalmus versions are usually better produced.

The other useful collection is the series of four volumes in much larger format—again Breitkopf-based—issued by Dover Publications in

New York. Three of these are in 9" x 12" format, and include respect-ively the piano sonatas and variations, the shorter piano works with opus numbers, and the transcriptions, exercises, and cadenzas for piano. The other is 8⅜" x 11¼", and contains the string quartets, quintets, and sextets and the Clarinet Quintet. All four are very well printed and, though paperbound, exceptionally sturdy.

Recommended Recordings

The criterion I have used in choosing recordings for this selective listing is essentially that of a really high performance standard. Mere adequacy, or ordinary professional competence, has not been considered a sufficient qualification. Thus, a number of works have been omitted from the list altogether when, although in some cases recordings exist, no available version seemed to me to meet the standard being applied. Moreover, the interests of the private record collector have been kept in mind rather than those of the scholar : a recorded version has been included only when, as the only version in a collection, it would in my view constitute a fully acceptable and representative statement of a given work, and such performances as Klemperer's and Karajan's of the symphonies and Rubinstein's of the piano concertos have therefore been omitted, although they would certainly command the attention of the researcher. *In line with this subjective approach, I have grouped the listed versions of each work in the order of my own personal preference.* The technical quality of all recordings included is of a good modern standard, except where the merit of a particular performance made it reasonable to discount this qualification, and such cases are noted in the appropriate place. Apart from this, the annotations to the list limit themselves to such factual matters as convenience of record layout, observance or omission of repeats, and, in the case of some classic performances, the personnel of chamber groups and the date of recording. Except for the general remarks on the piano music and the songs, whose inclusion below was prompted by special discographical considerations, all critical comment on the musical qualities of the recorded performances will be found in footnotes to the text in the main body of the book.

　　The inclusion of recordings is influenced neither by current avail-ability nor by convenience of coupling. Works coupled with the subject of a given recommendation are listed—in brackets—only when they are also by Brahms, and their inclusion does not constitute a recommendation unless they are also listed in their own sections.

NOTES

(a) Record numbers are for U.K. and U.S. releases only unless a recommended version is available solely in another country. Numbers are for U.K. releases unless otherwise specified, but where U.S. numbers are identical with U.K. numbers no separate indication is given. Older record numbers have been omitted where satisfactory modern pressings of the same performance exist.

(b) The abbreviation (M) indicates that a given performance is available in monophonic form only—in all other cases, records listed are stereophonic. (nas) indicates that discs in a multiple-record set are not available separately.

(c) All other abbreviations are self-explanatory, and the names of all performing groups are given in full on their first appearance in the list.

Symphonies

No. 1 in C minor

Horenstein—South West German Radio Symphony Orchestra.
  Vox 510 690.
Furtwängler—Vienna Philharmonic Orchestra.
  Unicorn WFS 6; (in set 1–4) Electrola Da Capo 1 C 147–50336–39—Germany (nas) (M).
Haitink—Concertgebouw Orchestra of Amsterdam.
  Philips 6500 519.
Boult—London Philharmonic Orchestra.
  EMI ASD 2871; (in set 1–4, Alto Rhapsody, overtures) SLS 5009.
Boult's performance is the only one of those listed to observe the first-movement repeat, which is also very rarely taken in concert performance. In his version, however, the orchestral sound, at least as recorded, is less

mellow than in the Horenstein and Haitink performances. Furtwängler's version is a studio recording made in 1947, and technically not remarkable for its date.

No. 2 in D major

Haitink—Concertgebouw.
   (*St. Antoni Variations*) Philips 6500 375.
Boult—LPO.
   (Alto Rhapsody) EMI ASD 2746; (in set 1–4, Alto Rhapsody, overtures) SLS 5009; US: Angel S–37032.
Furtwängler—Berlin Philharmonic Orchestra.
   (in set 1–4) Electrola Da Capo 1 C 147–50336–39—Germany (nas) (M).
Monteux—London Symphony Orchestra.
   (*Academic Festival Overture*) Philips 6580 054.
Ansermet—Suisse Romande Orchestra.
   (*Tragic Overture*) Decca SPA 379.
Walter—Columbia Symphony Orchestra.
   (*Tragic Overture*) CBS 61218; US: Columbia Odyssey Y–31924.
Boult, Monteux, and Ansermet take the first-movement repeat. The Furtwängler is a live performance given in Munich in 1952 and broadcast by Bayerischer Rundfunk; the recorded sound is fair for the period.

No. 3 in F major

Furtwängler—BPO.
   Unicorn WFS 4; (in set 1–4) Electrola Da Capo 1 C 147–50336–39—Germany (nas) (M).
Giulini—Philharmonia Orchestra.
   (*Tragic Overture*) EMI SAX 2516; US: Angel Seraphim S–60101.
Mengelberg—Concertgebouw.
   Germany: (*Academic Festival Overture*) Electrola Da Capo 1 C 053-01453 (M).
Boult—LSO.
   (*Tragic Overture*) EMI ASD 2660; (in set 1–4, Alto Rhapsody, overtures) SLS 5009.
Bernstein—New York Philharmonic.
   (in set 1–4) US: Columbia D3M 32097 (nas).
The Furtwängler is another live performance, recorded in Berlin in 1949;

the sound, technically, is the best in any of Furtwängler's Brahms symphony recordings, though there is a distracting amount of coughing from the audience. Considering its much earlier date—1932—the Mengelberg recording has even more remarkable sound and particularly clear textures. The Giulini performance (which, at the time of writing, is not available in Britain) is the only one of the five recommended to omit the first-movement repeat. In terms of format, Boult and Bernstein meet with very different treatment from their record companies: intelligently, EMI puts the overture at the beginning, so that there is no need to jump up hastily at the end of the symphony to take the record off; American Columbia, no doubt in quest of economy, couples the four symphonies inconveniently for collectors that do not use auto-changers—No. 3 is split over two discs.

No. 4 in E minor

Giulini—Chicago Symphony Orchestra.
> EMI ASD 2650; US: Angel S–36040.

Furtwängler—BPO.
> (Hungarian Dances) Unicorn WFS 1; (in set 1–4) Electrola Da Capo 1 C 147–50336–39—Germany (nas); US: Vox Turnabout 4476 (M).

Ansermet—Suisse Romande Orchestra.
> (*Academic Festival Overture*) Decca SPA 381.

Boult—LPO.
> (*Academic Festival Overture*) EMI ASD 2901; (in set 1–4, Alto Rhapsody, overtures) SLS 5009.

Haitink—Concertgebouw.
> Philips 6500 389.

Sawallisch—Vienna Symphony Orchestra.
> (*Academic Festival Overture*) Philips Universo 6580 024; US: (in set 1–4, St. Antoni Variations, overtures) Vox Turnabout S–34453–56 (nas).

The Furtwängler performance was recorded live in Berlin in 1948; technically it is fair for the period. In the Boult release, the overture is again intelligently placed at the beginning of the disc.

Concertos

Piano Concerto No. 1 in D minor

Brendel—Concertgebouw—Schmidt-Isserstedt.
　　Philips 6500 623.
Weissenberg—LSO—Giulini.
　　EMI ASD 2992; US: Angel S–36967.
Curzon—Concertgebouw—Van Beinum.
　　Decca LXT 2825 (M).
Arrau—Concertgebouw—Haitink.
　　(Piano Concerto No. 2) Philips 6700 018 (nas in Britain); US—also available separately: 6500 018.

Curzon's recording, though dating from the year 1953, still sounds remarkably good. This performance should not be confused with the rather less successful one he recorded later in stereo with George Szell and the London Symphony Orchestra.

Piano Concerto No. 2 in B flat major

Brendel—Concertgebouw—Haitink.
　　Philips 6500 767.
Backhaus—VPO—Schuricht.
　　Decca LXT 2723 (M); US: Vox Turnabout 34419E (electronic stereo).
Barenboim—New Philharmonia Orchestra—Barbirolli.
　　EMI ASD 2413; (with Piano Concerto No. 1) SLS 874; US: Angel S–36526.
E. Fischer—BPO—Furtwängler.
　　Unicorn UN 1102; US: Vox Turnabout 4342 (M).
Schnabel—BBC Symphony Orchestra—Boult.
　　World Record Club SH 109 (M).
Richter—Paris Orchestra—Maazel.
　　EMI ASD 2554; US: Angel S–36728.
Arrau—Philharmonia—Giulini.
　　EMI Classics for Pleasure CFP 40034; US: Angel Seraphim S–60052.

The Schnabel, Fischer (a broadcast performance), and Backhaus recordings date respectively from the years 1935, 1942 and 1952, but all three sound very good for their age. The Backhaus—much preferable in the mono press-

ing—is particularly well recorded, and should not be confused with the pianist's less successful performances with other conductors. Similarly, the Richter release listed is to be preferred to this pianist's earlier version with Erich Leinsdorf and the Chicago Symphony Orchestra.

Violin Concerto

Kreisler—LPO—Barbirolli.
   World Record Club SH 115 (electronic stereo).
Krebbers—Concertgebouw—Haitink.
   Philips Universo 6580 087.
Grumiaux—NPO—Davis.
   Philips 6500 299.
Menuhin—Lucerne Festival Orchestra—Furtwängler.
   EMI HLM 7015 (M).
Szigeti—Hallé Orchestra—Harty.
   US: Columbia M6X 51513 (M—6-record set nas).
Menuhin (1949), Kreisler (1936), and Szigeti (1928) are all excellent recordings for their date. Kreisler uses his own cadenza (chosen also by Menuhin) instead of the "standard" Joachim one.

Concerto for Violin, Cello, and Orchestra (Double Concerto)

Szeryng—Starker—Concertgebouw—Haitink.
   Philips 6500 137.

Other Orchestral Works

St. Antoni Variations

Monteux—LSO.
   Decca SPA 121; US: London STS 15188.

Casals—Marlboro Festival Orchestra

(Cello Sonata No. 2) US: Columbia M5–30069 (5-record set nas).

These are both good modern recordings, made towards the end of their conductors' lives. The Monteux, indeed, is one of the most spectacularly well recorded of all Brahms discs, with remarkable differentiation of instrumental timbres.

Academic Festival Overture

Boult—LPO.

(Symphony No. 4) EMI ASD 2901.

Monteux—LSO.

(Symphony No. 2) Philips 6580 054.

Mengelberg—Concertgebouw.

Germany: (Symphony No. 3) Electrola Da Capo 1 C 053-01453 (M).

The Electrola is a fairly crackly 1930 recording, but worth persevering with for the sake of a classic performance.

Tragic Overture

Boult—LSO.

(Symphony No. 3) EMI ASD 2660.

Giulini—Philharmonia.

(Symphony No. 3) EMI SAX 2516; US: Angel Seraphim S–60101.

Serenade No. 1 in D major

Brusilow—Chamber Symphony of Philadelphia.

RCA Victor SB 6754: US: LSC 2976.

Anshel Brusilow, conducting a thirty-six-player orchestra that had a short but brilliant history in the late Sixties, observes the first-movement repeat. The recording is outstanding.

Serenade No. 2 in A major

Bernstein—New York Phil.
    CBS 73197; US: Columbia MS 7132.
The recording is somewhat larger than life, in American Columbia's New York manner, but Bernstein's performance is itself spacious enough to survive unimpaired.

Chamber Music

String Quartet No. 1 in C minor, op. 51 No. 1

Cleveland Quartet.
    (in set 1–3) RCA Victor DPS 2050; US: VCS 7102 (nas).
Melos Quartet of Stuttgart.
    (String Quartet No. 3) Deutsche Grammophon 2530 345.
Fine Arts Quartet.
    (String Quartet No. 2) US: Concert-Disc CS–226.
All three recommended versions omit the first-movement repeat. In common with several sets of its kind, the RCA Cleveland Quartet recording splits the works most inconveniently for listeners with single-record players—the First Quartet has its first three movements on Side One of the first disc and its Finale on the second disc. The Fine Arts version, made when Irving Ilmer was the group's violist, has rather dry recorded sound. But in both cases the disadvantages are outweighed by the quality of performance.

String Quartet No. 2 in A minor, op. 51 No. 2

Cleveland Quartet.
    (in set 1–3) RCA Victor DPS 2050; US: VCS 7102 (nas).
Busch Quartet.
    Japan: EMI GR 2237 (M).
Fine Arts Quartet.
    (String Quartet No. 1) US: Concert-Disc CS–226.
The first-movement repeat is again omitted in all three versions. The Busch Quartet recording was made in 1947, with Ernest Drucker playing 2nd violin and Hugo Gottesmann viola; the sound is good, though marred by fairly heavy surface noise.

String Quartet No. 3 in B flat major, op. 67

Fine Arts Quartet.
    US: Everest 3266.
Cleveland Quartet.
    (in set 1–3) RCA Victor DPS 2050; US: VCS 7102 (nas).
Melos Quartet of Stuttgart.
    (String Quartet No. 1) Deutsche Grammophon 2530 345.
Again, no first-movement repeats. The Fine Arts Quartet made this recording two violists later in its history (with Bernard Zaslav) than that of the first two string quartets, and is helped also by better sound.

String Quintets No. 1 in F major, op. 88, and No. 2 in G major, op. 111

Members of Berlin Philharmonic Octet.
    Philips 6500 177.
The first-movement repeat is observed in the First Quintet; that of the Second Quintet is omitted.

String Sextet No. 1 in B flat major, op. 18

Stern—Schneider—Katims—Thomas—Casals—Foley.
  Philips GBL5623; US: Columbia M5X–32768 (5-record set nas) (M).
*Though recorded in the studio, this classic performance emanates from the
1952 Casals Festival at Prades, in the French Pyrenees. The first-movement
repeat is omitted.*

String Sextet No. 2 in G major, op. 36

Carmirelli—Toth—Naegele—Levine—Arico—Reichenberger.
  US: Columbia MS 7445.
*As with the recommended version of the First Sextet, this performance
combines the advantages of studio recording conditions with a background
of preparation and live performance at an actual music festival—in this
case, the 1970 Marlboro Festival in Vermont, U.S.A. All repeats in this
already spacious work are observed.*

Clarinet Quintet

Kell—Busch Quartet.
  Japan: EMI GR 2240 (M).
De Peyer—Melos Ensemble.
  EMI ASD 620; US: Angel S–36280.
Brymer—Prometheus Ensemble.
  Pye TPLS 13004.
Leister—Amadeus Quartet.
  Deutsche Grammophon 139 354.
*The first-movement repeat is omitted in the Kell/Busch performance, which
has good 1937 sound, but observed in the other three versions. The Busch
Quartet second violinist here is Gösta Andreasson and the violist Karl Doktor.*

Clarinet Trio

Honingh—Bylsma—Frager.
   (Horn Trio) US: BASF KMB 21184.
Leister—Donderer—Eschenbach.
   (Horn Trio) Deutsche Grammophon 139 398.

Horn Trio

A. Brain—Busch—Serkin.
   US: Angel Seraphim 6044 (3-record set nas); Japan: (Violin Sonata No.
   2) EMI GR 2242 (M).
Tuckwell—Perlman—Ashkenazy.
   Decca SXL 6408; US: London 6628.
Cicil—Y. Menuhin—H. Menuhin.
   (Piano Trio No. 2) US: Angel S–36472.
D. Brain—Salpeter—Preedy.
   BBC REB 175 (M).
Aubrey Brain's recording, which has served as a model to most horn-players since, was made in 1933. His son Dennis's is taken from a live broadcast made in February 1957, a few months before his death. All the listed performances observe the Finale repeat.

Piano Quartet No. 1 in G minor, op. 25

Szolchany—members of Hungarian Quartet.
   Germany: (in set 1–3, Piano Quintet, Schumann Variations op. 9,
   Scherzo op. 4) Electrola 1 C 163–10730–33 (nas).
Serkin—members of Busch Quartet.
   Japan: EMI GR 2238 (M).
The Serkin/Busch recording dates from 1949, when the quartet's violist was Hugo Gottesmann. The quality of the sound is very good, with much less surface noise than the other Busch Quartet and associated recordings listed in these pages. Both performances observe all repeats in the gypsy-style Finale.

Piano Quartet No. 2 in A major, op. 26

Babin—Goldberg—Primrose—Graudan.
  RCA Victor SB 6583; US: LSC 2517.
Serkin—members of Busch Quartet.
  Japan: EMI GR 2239 (M).
The Serkin/Busch recording is much older than that of the First Piano Quartet: it was made in 1932, when Karl Doktor was the group's violist, and the surface noise is fairly heavy. Both performances listed omit the first-movement repeat.

Piano Quartet No. 3 in C minor, op. 60

Aller—members of Hollywood Quartet.
  Capitol P 8379 (M).
Szolchany—members of Hungarian Quartet.
  Germany: (in set 1–3, Piano Quintet, Schumann Variations op. 9, Scherzo op. 4) Electrola 1 C 163–10730–33 (nas).

Piano Quintet

Richter—Beethoven Quartet.
  MK 1516 (M).
Previn—Yale Quartet.
  EMI ASD 2873; US: Angel S–36928.
Bauer—Flonzaley Quartet.
  US: RCA Victrola VCM 7103 (M—2-record set nas).
The Richter/Beethoven Quartet version is one of the best Soviet recordings from the end of the monophonic period. The Bauer/Flonzaley performance was recorded in 1925: it has reasonable sound, but is the only one of these three performances to omit the first-movement repeat.

Piano Trio No. 1 in B major, op. 8 (revised version)

Katchen—Suk—Starker.
(Piano Trio No. 3) Decca SXL 6387; US: London 6611.
Repeats are observed both in the first movement and in the Scherzo.

Piano Trio No. 2 in C major, op. 87

Serkin—A. Busch—H. Busch.
US: Columbia Odyssey 32 16 0361 (M).
Katchen—Suk—Starker.
(Cello Sonata No. 2) Decca SXL 6589; US: London 6814.
H. Menuhin—Y. Menuhin—Gendron.
(Horn Trio) US: Angel S–36472.
The Serkin/Busch version is an excellent 1951 recording. All three perform-
ances observe Scherzo repeats.

Piano Trio No. 3 in C minor, op. 101

Katchen—Suk—Starker.
(Piano Trio No. 1) Decca SXL 6387; US: London 6611.

Cello Sonata No. 1 in E minor, op. 38

Rostropovich—Richter.
US: Parnassus 2 (M).
Feuermann—Van der Pas.
US: Parnassus 1 (M).
Du Pré—Barenboim.
(Cello Sonata No. 2) EMI ASD 2436; US: Angel S–36544.
The first two versions listed were both released by a small American com-
pany: the Feuermann/Van der Pas issue has acceptable, if rather dry, Thirties
sound, whereas the Rostropovich/Richter, though monophonic, is a fairly

good modern recording. Of the repeats in the first and second movements, all are observed by Rostropovich/Richter, only those in the second movement by du Pré/Barenboim, and none by Feuermann/Van der Pas.

Cello Sonata No. 2 in F major, op. 99

Casals—Horszowski.
    US: (*St. Antoni Variations*) Columbia M5–30069 (M—5-record set nas).
Du Pré—Barenboim.
    (Cello Sonata No. 1) EMI ASD 2436; US: Angel S–36544.
Starker—Katchen.
    (Piano Trio No. 2) Decca SXL 6589; US: London 6814.
The Casals/Horszowski recording has exceptionally rich sound for its date of 1936. The three performances listed observe all repeats.

Clarinet Sonatas No. 1 in F minor and No. 2 in E flat major, op. 120
Nos. 1 and 2

original version:
De Peyer—Barenboim.
    EMI ASD 2362.

arrangement by Brahms for viola and piano:
Zukerman—Barenboim.
    (Violin Sonatas, "F-A-E" Scherzo) Deutsche Grammophon 2709 058 (nas).
Trampler—Horszowski.
    RCA Victor SB 6734; US: LSC 2933.
All performances observe the third-movement repeats in the F minor Sonata.

Violin Sonata No. 1 in G major, op. 78

Zukerman—Barenboim.
> (Violin Sonatas Nos. 2 and 3, "F-A-E" Scherzo, Clarinet Sonatas) Deutsche Grammophon 2709 058 (nas).

Wiłkomirska—Barbosa.
> US: (Violin Sonata No. 2) Connoisseur Society CS 2079.

Suk—Katchen.
> (Violin Sonatas Nos. 2 and 3) Decca SXL 6321; US: London 6549.

The last-named has what is technically perhaps the best recording of any of Katchen's Brahms releases, whether solo or in ensemble: the balance is exemplary, the piano sound well contained, and the violin tone silvery. The Zukerman/Barenboim set is equally well engineered, and perhaps even a shade more immediate; this sonata is spread over a side and a half.

Violin Sonata No. 2 in A major, op. 100

Suk—Katchen.
> (Violin Sonatas Nos. 1 and 3) Decca SXL 6321; US: London 6549.

Wiłkomirska—Barbosa.
> US: (Violin Sonata No. 1) Connoisseur Society CS 2079.

Zukerman—Barenboim.
> (Violin Sonatas Nos. 1 and 3, "F-A-E" Scherzo, Clarinet Sonatas) Deutsche Grammophon 2709 058 (nas).

Busch—Serkin.
> Japan: (Horn Trio) EMI GR 2242 (M).

The Suk/Katchen performance is split over the two sides of the disc, which is the understandable corollary of the economy of the coupling. The Busch/Serkin is a good 1932 recording.

Violin Sonata No. 3 in D minor, op. 108

D. Oistrakh—Richter.
> EMI ASD 2618; US: Melodiya/Angel S–40121.

Suk—Katchen.
> (Violin Sonatas Nos. 1 and 2) Decca SXL 6321; US: London 6549.

Wiłkomirska—Barbosa.
> US: Connoisseur Society CS 2080.

Zukerman—Barenboim.
> (Violin Sonatas Nos. 1 and 2, "F-A-E" Scherzo, Clarinet Sonatas) Deutsche Grammophon 2709 058 (nas).

The Oistrakh/Richter release is an outstanding example of what can be achieved, technically, with live recording of a concert performance.

Piano Music

Note: Two complete recordings of the original solo piano works exist. One, by Walter Klien, is officially available in the U.S. only (in two Vox Boxes, SVBX 5430 and 5431). The other, by Julius Katchen, is available both in the U.S. (on London CSP–5, 8 records, of which some are available separately) and in Britain (on Decca Ace of Diamonds, 9 records, available separately on the standard-price Decca SXL label); in addition to the original solo works, it includes Brahms's own solo arrangement of the first two sets of Hungarian dances, the third and fourth sets in their authentic duet form with Jean-Pierre Marty, and, in Britain, the three violin sonatas and the Scherzo, or *Sonatensatz*, for violin and piano with Josef Suk. (Neither set includes the many small solo exercises and other pieces without opus number or such arrangements as the Theme and Variations from the First Sextet—see below.)

Though the Klien set is only about half as expensive, either in the U.S. or from specialist dealers in Britain, the performances cannot in my view hold a candle to Katchen's, which are infinitely bolder, more imaginative, and more exciting. In the ensuing list of individual piano works I have included only three performances from the Katchen set—those of the first two piano sonatas and the Paganini Variations—and they are chosen because I find them outstanding even for Katchen. But where no recommended version of a work is included, a general recommendation of the Katchen performances should be assumed to apply.

Sonatas No. 1 in C major, op. 1, and No. 2 in F sharp minor, op. 2

Katchen.
    Decca SXL 6129; US: London 6410.
Katchen omits the exposition repeat in the first movement of the First Sonata, but observes that in the Finale of the Second.

Scherzo in E flat minor, op. 4, and Sonata No. 3 in F minor, op. 5

Arrau.
Philips 6500 377.
The recording is exceptionally rich and solid. Arrau observes all repeats in the first three movements of the Sonata and in the Scherzo.

Variations on a Theme by Schumann, op. 9

Barenboim.
(Handel Variations; Theme and Variations from Sextet No. 1) Deutsche Grammophon 2530 335.
This too is an outstanding solo piano recording remarkably clear in the bass and luminous in the higher registers.

Variations on an Original Theme, op. 21 No. 1

Vázsonyi.
(Fantasies, op. 116 Nos. 1–3; Piano Pieces, op. 119) Pye TPLS 13016.

Variations and Fugue on a Theme by Handel, op. 24

Barenboim.
(Schumann Variations; Theme and Variations from Sextet No. 1) Deutsche Grammophon 2530 335.
Bishop.
(Intermezzos, op. 117; Piano Pieces, op. 119) Philips SAL 3758; US: 839 722.
Solomon.
(Intermezzo, op. 117 No. 2) EMI RLS 701 (M—3-record set nas).
The virtues of Solomon's performance have to be perceived through a recording with an exceptional amount of surface hiss even for 1942.

Variations on a Theme by Paganini, op. 35, Books 1 and 2

Katchen.
　(Handel Variations) Decca SXL 6218; US: London STS 15150.

Fantasies, op. 116

Nos. 1–3:
Vázsonyi.
　(Variations on an Original Theme; Piano Pieces, op. 119) Pye TPLS 13016.

Three Intermezzos, op. 117

Bishop.
　(Handel Variations; Piano Pieces, op. 119) Philips SAL 3758; US: 839 722.
No. 2 only:
Moravec.
　US: (Intermezzo, op. 118 No. 2) Connoisseur Society CS 2062.

Six Piano Pieces, op. 118

No. 2 only:
Moravec.
　US: (Intermezzo, op. 117 No. 2) Connoisseur Society CS 2062.

Four Piano Pieces, op. 119

Bishop.

(Handel Variations; Intermezzos, op. 117) Philips SAL 3758; US: 839 722.
Vázsonyi.
(Variations on an Original Theme; Fantasies, op. 116 Nos. 1–3) Pye TPLS 13016.
The Philips recording wisely places opus 119 before opus 117 on the disc, so that the E flat major Rhapsody—the loudest piece in either set—is kept away from the inner grooves, where its sound would tend, as in the Vázsonyi release, to be slightly constricted. Both pianists take the repeat in No. 2.

Theme and Variations in D minor (arranged by Brahms from the second movement of String Sextet No. 1)

Barenboim.
(Schumann Variations; Handel Variations) Deutsche Grammophon 2530 335.

Music for Two Pianos

Sonata in F Minor, op. 34b (earlier version of the Piano Quintet)

Billard—Azaïs Piano Duo.
US: Philips World Series PHC 9067.
The first-movement repeat is omitted.

Organ Music

Eleven Chorale Preludes, op. 122
Obetz.
    US: Célèbre 8005.
In this recording, made on the Aeolian-Skinner organ of the Auditorium, Independence, Missouri, each Chorale Prelude is preceded by a performance (by the Auditorium Chorale) of the chorale it is based on.

Songs

Note: A different method of arrangement is used here from that found in the rest of the discography, since it would have been extremely wasteful of space to organise the listing of this most copious category of Brahms's output under the titles of individual songs. The basis of any extensive collection of Brahms songs is bound to be Dietrich Fischer-Dieskau's seven-record set, made with three pianists and embracing three-quarters of the songs. It is an outstanding set in every respect except—since the British release comes without English translations of the song-texts—that of presentation. The 149 songs included are listed below in the order in which they appear on the records, and this entry is supplemented by a listing of other especially recommended song performances, also arranged by record.

Fischer-Dieskau

with Moore:
Liebe und Frühling I (Wie sich Rebenranken schwingen), op. 3 no. 2; Liebe und Frühling II (Ich muss hinaus), op. 3 no. 3; In der Fremde, op. 3 no. 5; Lied (Lindes Rauschen in den Wipfeln), op. 3 no. 6; Nachtigallen schwingen, op. 6 no. 6; Parole, op. 7 no. 2; Anklänge, op. 7 no. 3; Der Kuss, op. 19 no. 1; In der Ferne, op. 19 no. 3; Wie rafft ich mich auf, op. 32 no. 1; Nicht mehr zu dir zu gehen, op. 32 no. 2; Ich schleich umher betrübt, op. 32 no. 3; Der Strom, der neben mir verrauschte, op. 32 no. 4; Wehe, so willst du mich wieder, op. 32 no. 5; Du sprichst, dass ich mich täuschte, op. 32 no. 6; Bitteres zu sagen denkst du, op. 32 no. 7; So stehn wir, ich und meine Weide, op. 32 no. 8; Wie bist du, meine Königin, op. 32 no. 9.

with Sawallisch:
Lied (Weit über das Feld), op. 3 no. 4; Der Frühling, op. 6 no. 2; Nach-
wirkung, op. 6 no. 3; Juchhe, op. 6 no. 4; Wie die Wolke nach der Sonne,
op. 6 no. 5; Treue Liebe, op. 7 no. 1; Volkslied (Die Schwälble ziehet), op. 7
no. 4; Heimkehr, op. 7 no. 6; Vor dem Fenster, op. 14 no. 1; Vom ver-
wundeten Knaben, op. 14 no. 2; Murrays Ermordung, op. 14 no. 3; Ein
Sonett, op. 14 no. 4; Trennung (Wach auf, wach auf), op. 14 no. 5; Gang
zur Liebsten, op. 14 no. 6; Ständchen (Gut Nacht), op. 14 no. 7; Sehnsucht
(Mein Schatz ist nicht da), op. 14 no. 8; Scheiden und Meiden, op. 19 no. 2;
An eine Aeolsharfe, op. 19 no. 5; Von ewiger Liebe, op. 43 no. 1; Die
Mainacht, op. 43 no. 2; Ich schell mein Horn, op. 43 no. 3; Die Kränze,
op. 46 no. 1; Magyarisch, op. 46 no. 2; Die Schale der Vergessenheit, op. 46
no. 3; An die Nachtigall, op. 46 no. 4; Botschaft, op. 47 no. 1; Liebesglut,
op. 47 no. 2; Sonntag, op. 47 no. 3; O liebliche Wangen, op. 47 no. 4; Der
Gang zum Liebchen, op. 48 no. 1; Der Ueberläufer, op. 48 no. 2; Trost in
Tränen, op. 48 no. 5; Vergangen ist mir Glück und Heil, op. 48 no. 6;
Herbstgefühl, op. 48 no. 7; Am Sonntag Morgen, op. 49 no. 1; An ein
Veilchen, op. 49 no. 2; Sehnsucht (Hinter jenen dichten Wäldern), op. 49
no. 3; Wiegenlied (Guten Abend, gut Nacht), op. 49 no. 4; Abenddämmerung,
op. 49 no. 5; Wenn du nur zuweilen lächelst, op. 57 no. 2; Es träumte mir,
op. 57 no. 3; Ach, wende diesen Blick, op. 57 no. 4; In meiner Nächte Sehnen,
op. 57 no. 5; Strahlt zuweilen auch ein mildes Licht, op. 57 no. 6; Die Schnur,
die Perl an Perle, op. 57 no. 7; Unbewegte laue Luft, op. 57 no. 8; Blinde
Kuh, op. 58 no. 1; Während des Regens, op. 58 no. 2; Die Spröde, op 58 no. 3;
O komme, holde Sommernacht, op. 58 no. 4; Schwermut, op. 58 no. 5;
In der Gasse, op. 58 no. 6; Vorüber, op. 58 no. 7; Serenade (Leise, um dich
nicht zu wecken), op. 58 no. 8; Dämmerung senkte sich von oben, op 59 no. 1;
Auf dem See (Blauer Himmel, blaue Wogen), op. 59 no. 2; Regenlied (Walle,
Regen, walle nieder), op. 59 no. 3; Nachklang, op. 59 no. 4; Eine gute Nacht,
op. 59 no. 6; Mein wundes Herz verlangt nach Dir, op. 59 no. 7; Dein blaues
Auge, op. 59 no. 8; Frühlingstrost, op. 63 no. 1; Erinnerung, op. 63 no. 2; An
ein Bild, op. 63 no. 3; An die Tauben, op. 63 no. 4; Junge Lieder I (Meine Liebe
ist grün), op. 63 no. 5; Junge Lieder II (Wenn um den Hollunder), op. 63 no. 6;
Heimweh I (Wie traulich war), op. 63 no. 7; Heimweh II (O wüsst ich doch
den Weg zurück), op. 63 no. 8; Heimweh III (Ich sah als Knabe Blumen
blühn), op. 63 no. 9; Beim Abschied, op. 95 no. 3; Es schauen die Blumen,
op. 96 no. 3; Nachtigall (O Nachtigall, dein süsser Schall), op. 97 no. 1; Auf
dem Schiffe, op. 97 no. 2; Entführung, op. 97 no. 3; Komm bald, op. 97 no. 5;
Trennung (Da unten im Tale), op. 97 no. 6; Wie Melodien zieht es mir,
op. 105 no. 1; Klage (Feins Liebchen), op. 105 no. 3; Auf dem Kirchhofe,
op. 105 no. 4; Verrat, op. 105 no. 5; Ständchen (Der Mond steht über dem
Berge), op. 106 no. 1; Auf dem See (An dies Schifflein), op. 106 no. 2; Es hing
der Reif, op. 106 no. 3; Meine Lieder, op. 106 no. 4; Ein Wanderer, op. 106
no. 5; An die Stolze, op. 107 no. 1; Der Salamander, op. 107 no. 2; Maien-
kätzchen, op. 107 no. 4; Mondnacht; Vier ernste Gesänge, op. 121 (no. 1:
Denn es gehet dem Menschen wie dem Vieh; no. 2: Ich wandte mich und
sahe an alle; no. 3: O Tod, wie bitter bist du; no. 4: Wenn ich mit Menschen-
und mit Engelszungen redete).

with Barenboim:
Abschied, op. 69 no. 3; Tambourliedchen, op. 69 no. 5; Ueber die See, op. 69 no. 7; Im Garten, op. 70 no. 1; Lerchengesang, op. 70 no. 2; Serenade (Lieb-liches Kind, kannst du mir sagen), op. 70 no. 3; Abendregen, op. 70 no. 4; Es liebt sich so lieblich, op. 71 no. 1; An den Mond, op. 71 no. 2; Geheimnis, op. 71 no. 3; Willst du, dass ich geh, op. 71 no. 4; Minnelied, op. 71 no. 5; Alte Liebe, op. 72 no. 1; Sommerfäden, op. 72 no. 2; O kühler Wald, op. 72 no. 3; Verzagen, op. 72 no. 4; Unüberwindlich, op. 72 no. 5; Sommerabend (Dämmernd liegt der Sommerabend), op. 85 no. 1; Mondenschein, op. 85 no. 2; Ade!, op. 85 no. 4; Frühlingslied, op. 85 no. 5; In Waldeseinsamkeit, op. 85 no. 6; Therese, op. 86 no. 1; Feldeinsamkeit, op. 86 no. 2; Nacht-wandler, op. 86 no. 3; Ueber die Heide, op. 86 no. 4; Versunken, op. 86 no. 5; Todessehnen, op. 86 no. 6; Mit vierzig Jahren, op. 94 no. 1; Steig auf, geliebter Schatten, op. 94 no. 2; Mein Herz ist schwer, op. 94 no. 3; Kein Haus, keine Heimat, op. 94 no. 5; Bei dir sind meine Gedanken, op. 95 no. 2; Schön war, das ich dir weihte, op. 95 no. 7; Der Tod, das ist die kühle Nacht, op. 96 no. 1; Wir wandelten, op. 96 no. 2; Meerfahrt, op. 96 no. 4.
    EMI SLS 5002 (7-record set nas).
The two songs (Liebe und Frühling I, op. 3 no. 2, and Beim Abschied, op. 95 no. 3) that have come down in alternative versions are both performed in this set in their second versions. It should also be noted that the opus numbers of Die Schale der Vergessenheit *and* An die Nachtigall *are as given above (op. 46 no. 3 and op. 46 no. 4), and not as listed in the EMI booklet; the record label has them correctly.*

Fischer-Dieskau—Demus:

Sommerabend (Dämmernd liegt der Sommerabend), op. 85 no. 1; Monden-schein, op. 85 no. 2; Es liebt sich so lieblich, op. 71 no. 1; Meerfahrt, op. 96 no. 4; Es schauen die Blumen, op. 96 no. 3; Der Tod, das ist die kühle Nacht, op. 96 no. 1.
    Deutsche Grammophon LPM 18 370 (M).

Fischer-Dieskau—Klust:

Wie rafft ich mich auf in der Nacht, op. 32 no. 1; Nicht mehr zu dir zu gehen, op. 32 no. 2; Ich schleich umher betrübt und stumm, op. 32 no. 3; Der Strom, der neben mir verrauschte, op. 32 no. 4; Du sprichst, dass ich

mich täuschte, op. 32 no. 6; Wehe, so willst du mich wieder, op. 32 no. 5; Wie bist du, meine Königin, op. 32 no. 9.
EMI ALP 1270; US: Angel 35522 (M).

Fischer-Dieskau—Demus:

Mit vierzig Jahren, op. 94 no. 1; Steig auf, geliebter Schatten, op. 94 no. 2; Mein Herz ist schwer, op. 94 no. 3; Kein Haus, keine Heimat, op. 94 no. 5; Herbstgefühl, op. 48 no. 7; Alte Liebe, op. 72 no. 1; Abenddämmerung, op. 49 no. 5; Heimweh II (O wüsst ich doch den Weg zurück), op. 63 no. 8; Auf dem Kirchhofe, op. 105 no. 4; Verzagen, op. 72 no. 4; Regenlied (Walle, Regen, walle nieder), op. 59 no. 3; Nachklang, op. 59 no. 4; Frühlingslied, op. 85 no. 5; Auf dem See (Blauer Himmel, blaue Wogen), op. 59 no. 2; Feldeinsamkeit, op. 86 no. 2.
Deutsche Grammophon SLPM 138 011.

Fischer-Dieskau—Richter:

Romances from Tieck's *Magelone*, op. 33—no. 1: Keinen hat es noch gereut; no. 2: Traun! Bogen und Pfeil; no. 3: Sind es Schmerzen, sind es Freuden; no. 4: Liebe kam aus fernen Landen; no. 5: So willst du des Armen; no. 6: Wie soll ich die Freude; no. 7: War es dir, dem diese Lippen bebten; no. 8: Wir müssen uns trennen; no. 9: Ruhe, Süssliebchen; no. 10: Verzweiflung; no. 11: Wie schnell verschwindet; no. 12: Muss es eine Trennung geben; no. 13: Sulima; no. 14: Wie froh und frisch; no. 15: Treue Liebe dauert lange.
EMI Angel SAN 291; US: Angel S–36753.

Fischer-Dieskau—Barenboim:

Vier ernste Gesänge, op. 121.
(*Ein deutsches Requiem*) Deutsche Grammophon 2707 066 (nas).

Hotter—Moore.

Feldeinsamkeit, op. 86 no. 2; Mit vierzig Jahren, op. 94 no. 1; Vier ernste Gesänge, op. 121.
   Germany: Electrola Da Capo 1 C 147-01633/34 (M—2-record set nas).

Hotter—Moore.

Wie Melodien zieht es, op. 105 no. 1; Sonntag, op. 47 no. 3; Minnelied, op. 71 no. 5; Komm bald, op. 97 no. 5; Wir wandelten, op. 96 no. 2; Wie bist du, meine Königin, op. 32 no. 9; Sapphische Ode, op. 94 no. 4; Botschaft, op. 47 no. 1; Sommerabend (Dämmernd liegt der Sommerabend), op. 85 no. 1; Mondenschein, op. 85 no. 2; Ständchen (Der Mond steht über dem Berge), op. 106 no. 1; Heimweh II (O wüsst ich doch den Weg zurück), op. 63 no. 8; Auf dem Kirchhofe, op. 105 no. 4; Heimkehr, op. 7 no. 6; In Waldeseinsamkeit, op. 85 no. 6; Wenn du nur zuweilen lächelst, op. 57 no. 2; Verrat, op. 105 no. 5.
   EMI Columbia 33 CX 1448 (M).
All these Hotter/Moore recordings date from near the end of the monophonic period, and the sound is excellent.

Lehmann

with Ulanowsky:
Zigeunerlieder (Gypsy Songs), op. 103 (arranged by Brahms from the original version for vocal quartet and piano)—no. 1: He, Zigeuner; no. 2: Hochgetürmte Rimaflut; no. 3: Wisst ihr, wann mein Kindchen; no. 4: Lieber Gott, du weisst; no. 5: Brauner Bursche; no. 6: Röslein dreie; no. 7: Kommt dir manchmal in den Sinn; no. 11: Rote Abendwolken ziehn. Feldeinsamkeit, op. 86 no. 2; Der Kranz, op. 84 no. 2; Der Schmied, op. 19 no. 4.

with Balogh:
Der Tod, das ist die kühle Nacht, op. 96 no. 1; Therese, op. 86 no. 1; Meine Liebe ist grün, op. 63 no. 5; Botschaft, op. 47 no. 1; Das Mädchen spricht,

op. 107 no. 3; Mein Mädel hat einen Rosenmund, 49 Deutsche Volkslieder, book IV no. 25.

US: RCA Victrola VIC 1320 (M—also released in electronic stereo).
Both voice and piano are reproduced vividly enough in these recordings. But even the performances with Paul Ulanowsky, recorded in 1947, have been transferred with a good deal of the original surface noise: the recordings with Ernő Balogh, of which the first three date from 1935 and the others from 1937, are scarcely inferior technically. The monophonic pressing is recommended in preference to the electronic stereo.

Kipnis—Moore.

Vier ernste Gesänge, op. 121.
EMI HLM 7040; US: Angel Seraphim 60076 (M).
This is a 1936 recording but the transfer is exceptionally skilful and the sound quite free from extraneous noise.

De los Angeles—Moore.

Sapphische Ode, op. 94 no. 4; Der Gang zum Liebchen, op. 48 no. 1; Vergebliches Ständchen, op. 84 no. 4.
EMI Angel SAN 182–83; US: Angel SB–3697 (2-record set nas).
These recordings were made in 1967 at a London concert in honour of Gerald Moore. The group is punctuated by a quantity of applause, but the audience is almost completely quiet during the songs themselves, and the technical quality is excellent.

Schlusnus—Peschko—Rupp.

Botschaft, op. 47 no. 1; Wie bist du, meine Königin, op. 32 no. 9; Der Gang zum Liebchen, op. 48 no. 1; Die Mainacht, op. 43 no. 2; Am Sonntag Morgen, op. 49 no. 1; Feldeinsamkeit, op. 86 no. 2; Wenn du nur zuweilen lächelst, op. 57 no. 2; Tambourliedchen, op. 69 no. 5; Ständchen (Der Mond steht

über dem Berge), op. 106 no. 1; Von ewiger Liebe, op. 43 no. 1.
  Heliodor 2548 720 (M).
Though these recordings qualify in at least one sense as historical—Schlusnus died in 1952—they do not sound it: the engineering, as in the Kipnis disc listed above, has been very well managed.

Vocal Ensembles

Four Duets for alto, baritone, and piano, op. 28

Baker—Fischer-Dieskau—Barenboim.
  EMI ASD 2555; US: Angel S–36712.
These live recordings from a 1969 London concert are reasonably well balanced. Applause is heard only at the end of the group, and the audience is otherwise very quiet. The only sign of concert conditions in the performances themselves is a curious rhythmic inaccuracy near the end of the third duet (Es rauschet das Wasser) which would probably have been corrected in a studio recording.

Liebeslieder (Love Songs), op. 52, and Neue Liebeslieder (New Love Songs), op. 65—waltzes for vocal quartet and piano duet

Morison—Thomas—Lewis—Bell—Vronsky & Babin.
  EMI ALP 1789 (M); US: Angel Seraphim S–60033.

Choral Music

Begräbnisgesang (Funeral Hymn) for chorus, wind instruments, and timpani, op. 13

Mácal—Czech Philharmonic Chorus and Orchestra.
  Czechoslovakia: (Alto Rhapsody; *St. Antoni Variations*) Supraphon SUA ST 50772.

Ein deutsches Requiem (A German Requiem), op. 45

Mathis—Fischer-Dieskau—Edinburgh Festival Chorus—LPO—Barenboim.
  (*Vier ernste Gesänge*) Deutsche Grammophon 2707 066.
Giebel—Prey—Suisse Romande and Lausanne Pro Arte Choirs—Suisse Romande Orch—Ansermet.
  (Alto Rhapsody; *Nänie*) Decca SET 333–34; US: London 1265.
Lindberg-Torlind—Sonnestedt—Stockholm Phil Chorus and Orch—Furtwängler.
  Unicorn WFS 17–18 (M).
The Furtwängler set was recorded—and rather dimly—at a public performance in 1948.

Alto Rhapsody, op. 53

Baker—John Alldis Choir—LPO—Boult.
  (Symphony No. 2) EMI ASD 2746; (in set Symphonies 1–4, overtures) SLS 5009; US: Angel S–37032.
Soukupová—Czech Phil Chorus and Orch—Mácal.
  Czechoslovakia: (*Begräbnisgesang; St. Antoni Variations*) Supraphon SUA ST 50772.
Watts—Suisse Romande and Lausanne Pro Arte Choirs—Suisse Romande Orch—Ansermet.
  (*Ein deutsches Requiem; Nänie*) Decca SET 333–34; US: London 1265.

Schicksalslied (Song of Destiny), op. 54

Abbado—Ambrosian Chorus—NPO.
(*Rinaldo*) Decca SXL 6386; US: London 26106.
This is a more successful recording than that of the cantata Rinaldo, *with which it is coupled.*

Nänie (Lament), op. 82

Ansermet—Suisse Romande and Lausanne Pro Arte Choirs and Suisse Romande Orch.
(*Ein deutsches Requiem*; Alto Rhapsody) Decca SET 333–34; US: London 1265.

Selected Choral Works

Schaffe in mir, Gott, op. 29 no. 2; Abendständchen, op. 42 no. 1; Vineta, op. 42 no. 2; Nun stehn die Rosen in Blute, op. 44 no. 7; Die Berge sind spitz, op. 44 no. 8; Am Wildbach die Weiden, op. 44 no. 9; Und gehst du über den Kirchhof, op. 44 no. 10; Waldesnacht, op. 62 no. 3; Warum ist das Licht gegeben? op. 74 no. 1; Fahr wohl, op. 93a no. 4; Nachtwache I (Leise Töne der Brust), op. 104 no. 1; Nachtwache II (Ruhn sie?), op. 104 no. 2; Fest- und Gedenksprüche, op. 109.
Jürgens—Monteverdi Choir, Hamburg (with Dieter Einfeldt, piano, in op. 42 no. 2 and op. 44 nos. 7–10).
   Telefunken SMT 1288.

Chronological Chart
of Brahms's Compositions

On the following pages I have attempted to provide a visual guide to the distribution of various musical *genres* throughout Brahms's working career. Works are listed—as accurately as the evidence permits—under their year of completion, and are arranged chronologically within that year. Spacing, however, within any one year should not be taken to imply exact times of completion. Arrows show the period of gestation of certain works, and start in the earliest year for which there is firm evidence that Brahms was engaged on composition. But given his methods, we can never be sure that sketching did not begin earlier than indicated.

Two works not included overleaf, because no firm dates can be assigned, are: the song *Regenlied (Regentropfen aus den Bäumenfallen—* not to be confused with the other *Regenlied*, op. 59 no. 3); the choral setting of Schiller's *Dem dunkeln Schoss der heil'gen Erde.*

Year	Orchestral Works	Chamber Music	Keyboard Music	Songs	Other Vocal
1849			Fantasia on a popular waltz		
1850					
1851		Piano Trio in A minor (uncertain authenticity and date)	Scherzo in E flat minor		
1852			Piano Sonata No.2		
1853		*Sonatensatz* for violin and piano	Piano Sonata No.1 Piano Sonata No.3 Variations on a Hungarian Theme	Six Songs, op. 3 Six Songs, op. 6 Six Songs, op. 7	
1854		Piano Trio No.1 (see also 1891)	Variations on a Theme of Schumann Four Ballades, op. 10		
1855			Two Gigues Two Sarabandes		
1856			Prelude and Fugue No.1 for organ		

1857			Variations on an Original Theme Prelude and Fugue No.2 for organ Fugue in A flat minor for organ Chorale Prelude and Fugue, *O Traurigkeit*, for organ		
1858	Serenade No.1 Piano Concerto No.1			Eight Songs and Romances, op. 14 (approximate date)	*Ave Maria* *Begräbnisgesang*
1859	Serenade No.2 (revised 1875)			Five Poems, op. 19	*Marienlieder* (approximate date) Psalm No. 13 (approximate date) Three Sacred Choruses (Nos. 1 and 2) (see also 1863)
1860		Sextet No.1			Partsongs, op. 17 Three Duets, op.20 (approx. date) Two Motets, op.29 (or earlier) Sacred Song, op.30 (approximate date) Three Partsongs, op. 42
1861		Piano Quartet No.1 (begun earlier)	Schumann Variations, for piano duet Handel Variations and Fugue		
1862		Piano Quartet No.2	Paganini Studies (Variations)		Four duets, op. 28 Five partsongs, op.41
1863		Piano Quintet	Sonata in F minor for two pianos		Three Quartets, with piano (approx. date) Three Sacred Choruses, op. 37 (No.3) (see also 1859)
1864				Nine Songs, op.32 (approximate date)	

Two Motets, op. 74 (No. 3) (approximate date: see also 1877)

Twelve Songs and Romances, op. 44 (begun earlier)

Ein deutsches Requiem

Rinaldo, Cantata

Liebeslieder (approximate date)

Alto *Rhapsodie*

Schicksalslied

Triumphlied

begun earlier

Fifteen Romances from *Magelone*
Four Songs, op. 43
Four Songs, op. 46
Five Songs, op. 47
Seven Songs, op. 48
Five Songs, op. 49

Eight Songs, op. 57
Eight Songs, op. 58

Sixteen Waltzes for piano duet

Sextet No.2
Cello Sonata No.1
Horn Trio

1865
1866
1867
1868
1869
1870
1871
1872

1873	St. Antoni Variations	String Quartet No.1 String Quartet No.2	St. Antoni Variations for two pianos	Eight Songs, op.59 Five Songs for Ophelia	
1874				Nine Songs, op.63	Three Quartets, with piano, op.64 (or earlier) Neue Liebeslieder (or earlier) Four Duets, op. 61 Seven Partsongs, op. 62 Five Duets, op.66 (approx. date) Kleine Hochzeitskantate
1875		Piano Quartet No.3			
1876	Symphony No.1	String Quartet No.3			
1877	Symphony No.2			Nine Songs, op.69 Four Songs, op.70 Five Songs, op.71 Five Songs, op.72	Two Motets, op. 74 (No.1) (see also 1865)
1878	Violin Concerto	Violin Sonata No.1	Eight Pieces, op. 76 (or earlier)	Six Songs, op. 86	Four Ballads and Romances, op. 75
1879			Two Rhapsodies, op.79	Six Songs, op. 85 (approximate date)	
1880	Academic Festival Overture Tragic Overture				

1881	Piano Concerto No.2	Five Romances and Songs, op. 84 (approximate date)	*Nänie*
1882	String Quintet No.1, Piano Trio No.2		*Gesang der Parzen*
1883	Symphony No.3		
1884		Two Songs with viola op. 91 (or earlier), Five Songs, op. 94, Seven Songs, op. 95	Four Quartets, with piano, op. 92, Six Songs and Romances, op. 93a, *Tafellied*, op. 93b
1885	Symphony No.4		
1886	Cello Sonata No.2, Violin Sonata No.2, Piano Trio No.3	Four Songs, op.96 (approximate date), Six Songs, op.97, Five Songs, op.105 (approximate date)	
1887	Double Concerto		*Zigeunerlieder*
1888	Violin Sonata No.3		Thirteen Canons for female voices (begun earlier), Five Partsongs, op.104

1889	Fest- und Gedenksprüche, op.109; Three Motets, op.110; Five Songs, op. 106; Five Songs, op.107
1890	String Quintet No.2
1891	Six Quartets, with piano, op. 112; Clarinet Trio; Clarinet Quintet; Piano Trio No.1, revised version (see also 1854)
1892	Fantasias, op. 116; Three Intermezzi, op. 117
1893	Fifty-One Exercises; Six Pieces, op. 118; Four Pieces, op. 119
1894	Clarinet Sonata No.1; Clarinet Sonata No.2
1895	Eleven Chorale Preludes, for organ (begun earlier)
1896	*Vier ernste Gesänge*

Index of Brahms's Works

Symphonies

Italics denotes a main reference
f=footnote

Symphonies   68f, 82, 115, 135, 179
No. 1 in C minor, op. 68   26, 57–60,
    89, 94–5, 100–101, 104–5,
    106, 109, 119, 124, 144,
    147, 160
No. 2 in D major, op. 73   22, 41–4,
    46–8, 62, 101–05, 113, 115,
    118, 119, 122, 148, 166

No. 3 in F major, op. 90   68f, 90–91,
    113–14, 118, 119–120, 152,
    160–68
No. 4 in E minor, op. 98   22, 31, 34,
    35, 89, 96–8, 110–11, 113,
    115, 119–20, 121, 123–4, 125,
    149

Concertos

Piano Concerto No. 1 in D minor, op. 15
    21, 70, 105–6, 109, 122, 144,
    152–60, 163
Piano Concerto No. 2 in B flat major,
    op. 83   17, 22, 45, 46, 48–51,
    62, 106, 118, 120, 125, 144,
    148, 153

Violin Concerto in D major, op. 77
    22, 60, 68f, 114, 122, 131f
Concerto in A minor, op. 102, for violin,
    cello, and orchestra (Double Concerto)
    22, 110, 115, 116, 120, 144,
    153

Other Orchestral Works

St. Antoni Variations, op. 56a   15, 108,
    110, 113, 115, 117, 179
Academic Festival Overture, op. 80
    22, 111, 115, 121
Tragic Overture, op. 81   22,
    121–2, 124, 148

Serenade No. 1 in D major, op. 11, for
    full orchestra   27–29, 52, 53,
    54, 71–2, 92–3, 98–9, 108,
    117, 119, 143, 148
Serenade No. 2 in A major, op. 16, for
    small orchestra   109, 116

Chamber Music

String Quartets   26, 146–7, 179, 180
No. 1 in C minor, op. 51 no. 1
    26, 46, 64–6, 79, 149
No. 2 in A minor, op. 51 no. 2
    55–7, 131–2, 144
No. 3 in B flat major, op. 67   22, 64,
    66–8, 131–2, 148–9
String Quintets   180
No. 1 in F major, op. 88   35, 149
No. 2 in G major, op. 111   22
String Sextets   180
No. 1 in B flat major, op. 18   30, 31,
    53–5, 88, 93–4, 110, 120
No. 2 in G major, op. 36   32, 32f,
    75–7
Clarinet Quintet in B minor, op. 115
    22, 116, 152, 168–173, 180
Trio in A minor, op. 114, for piano,
   clarinet, and cello   22, 63,
    80–81, 116, 125, 150–51
Trio in E flat major, op. 40, for piano,
   violin, and horn   41, 55–6, 62,
    91, 108, 116, 144

Piano Quartets
No. 1 in G minor, op. 25   72–3,
    83, 98, 106, 125
No. 2 in A major, op. 26   73, 106,
    130, 145
No. 3 in C minor, op. 60   22, 34,
    63–4, 149
Piano Quintet in F minor, op. 34
    32–3, 62, 73–4, 87, 106, 108
Piano Trios
No. 1 in B major, op. 8   19, 91–2,
    144, 179
No. 2 in C major, op. 87   144
No. 3 in C minor, op. 101   22, 80,
    120–21, 125, 144
Cello Sonatas   116
No. 1 in E minor, op. 38   15, 70
No. 2 in F major, op. 99   22, 34, 144
Clarinet Sonatas, op. 120   22, 109, 116
No. 1 in F minor   60, 61
No. 2 in E flat major   144
Violin Sonatas   26, 116
No. 2 in A major, op. 100   22
No. 3 in D minor, op. 108   22

Piano Music

Piano Music   26, 180
Sonata No. 1 in C major, op. 1
    19, 27, 127
Sonata No. 2 in F sharp minor, op. 2
    18, 19
Sonata No. 3 in F minor, op. 5
    19, 83–7, 149
Scherzo in E flat minor, op. 4   18, 19
Variations on a Theme of Schumann,
   op. 9   70

Variations and Fugue on a Theme of
   Handel, op. 24   30–31, 70
Studies (Variations) on a Theme of
   Paganini, op. 35 (two sets)   30–31
Intermezzo in B flat minor, op. 117
   no. 2   111–12
Six Pieces, op. 118   22
Four Pieces, op. 119   22
Fantasia on a popular waltz   18
Sarabande in A minor (1855)   35

Music for Two Pianos

Sonata in F minor, op. 34b   108   *St. Antoni Variations*, op. 56b   108

Organ Music

Fugues 70

Eleven Chorale Preludes, op. 122
35, 70–71

Songs

Opus 3 19
Liebestreu, op. 3 no. 1 128
Liebe und Frühling I, op. 3 no. 2 131
Lied (Weit über das Feld), op. 3 no. 4 131
Opus 6 19
Von ewiger Liebe, op. 43 no. 1 135–7
Die Mainacht, op. 43 no. 2 138–9
Abendregen, op. 70 no. 4 149–50
In Waldeseinsamkeit, op. 85 no. 6 132–3
Feldeinsamkeit, op. 86 no. 2 111–12, 139

Beim Abschied, op. 95 no. 3 132–3
Ständchen (Der Mond steht über dem Berge), op. 106 no. 1 129–130, 134
Vier ernste Gesänge, op. 121 128
no. 1: Denn es gehet dem Menschen 140
no. 3: O Tod, wie bitter bist du 139–140, 149
Mondnacht (? 1854) 128–9
Five Songs for Ophelia (1873) 179
Deutsche Volkslieder 22, 127
Book VII, no. 49: Verstohlen geht der Mond auf 127–8

Vocal Ensembles

Es rauschet das Wasser, op. 28 no. 3 63f
Liebeslieder, op. 52, waltzes for vocal quartet with piano duet 127

Neue Liebeslieder, op. 65, waltzes for vocal quartet with piano duet 127
Zigeunerlieder, op. 103, for vocal quartet and piano 22

Choral Music

Choral Music 127
Begräbnisgesang, op. 13, for chorus, wind instruments, and timpani 140
Ein deutsches Requiem, op. 45 21, 26, 70, 78–9, 109, 115, 116, 117, 119, 125, 144
Gesang der Parzen, op. 89 179

General Index

Discography references have *not* been indexed. f=footnote.

Ansermet, Ernest   14, 36f
Arrau, Claudio   52f

Babin, Victor   145f
Bach, Carl Philipp Emanuel   105
—— Symphony in D major   34
Bach, Johann Sebastian   14, 17, 18, 24, 25, 30, 32, 34, 36, 71

—— Cantata No. 150   31
Bach, Wilhelm Friedemann   24
Bad Ischl   22, 23
Baker, Janet   63f
Barbi, Alice   20
Barenboim, Daniel   61f, 63f
Bartók, Béla   38, 106
Beethoven, Ludwig van   14, 17, 24, 26, 30, 32, 36f, 37, 40–41, 78, 87–8, 106, 109, 115, 142, 144, 174
—— *Missa Solemnis*   24, 40
—— Piano Concerto No. 1   153
—— Piano Concerto No. 2   153
—— Piano Concerto No. 3   153
—— Piano Concerto No. 4   153
—— Piano Concerto No. 5   106, 145–6, 153
—— "Waldstein" Piano Sonata   18
—— "Hammerklavier" Piano Sonata   27
—— "Archduke" Piano Trio   87
—— Quartet No. 14 op. 131   34
—— Quartet No. 15, op. 132   24
—— Quintet, op. 16   17
—— Septet in E flat major   27, 30
—— Symphony No. 1   27
—— Symphony No. 2   27
—— Symphony No. 3   116

—— Symphony No. 4   87–8
—— Symphony No. 5   30, 31
—— Symphony No. 7   39
—— Symphony No. 8   40, 42
—— Symphony No. 9   115
—— Violin Concerto   115
—— Violin Sonata No. 5   27
Berg, Alban   106
Berlin Philharmonic Orchestra   113f
Berlioz, Hector   19, 109, 122
Bernstein, Leonard   14
Billroth, Theodor   23
Bonn   19, 23
Boult, Sir Adrian   14, 36f 43f
Brahms, Caroline   21
—— Christine   16, 20, 21
—— Elise   16, 17
—— Eritz Friedrich   16
—— Johann Jakob   16, 17, 21, 118
Breitkopf & Härtel   19, 179
Bremen   26
Brendel, Alfred   45f, 52f
Breslau, University of   22
Britten, Benjamin   15
Bruckner, Anton   77, 146
Brusilow, Anshel   71f, 117f
Bruyr, José   178
Bülow, Hans von   31
Busch Quartet   145f

Carlsbad   23
Carmina Burana (anon.)   38
Carter, Elliott   38
—— Cello Sonata (1948)   51–2
Casals, Pablo   120f

Chamber Symphony of Philadelphia
117f
Chesterfield, Lord   22
Chopin, Frédéric   39
Cleveland Quartet   46f
Concertgebouw Orchestra, Amsterdam
52f
Cossel, Friedrich Wilhelm   17
Cranz   18

Detmold   21, 25
Donizetti, Gaetano
—— Una furtiva lagrima (from L'elisir
d'amore   131f
Dowland, John   139
Düsseldorf   19
Dvořák, Antonín   23, 46, 99
—— Cello Concerto   120
—— Symphony No. 7   45–6

Elgar, Sir Edward
—— Symphony No. 2   160
Endenich   19
Evans, Edwin   178

Fine Arts Quartet   66f
Fischer-Dieskau, Dietrich   63f, 134f
Franck, César
—— Symphony in D minor   90
Frankfurt-am-Main   23
Fuller-Maitland, J. A.   14
Furtwängler, Wilhelm   14, 36f, 68, 113f

Gál, Hans   177, 179
Geiringer, Karl   177, 179
Gesellschaft der Musikfreunde, Vienna
21
Gewandhaus, Leipzig   19
Giesemann, Adolf   18f
—— Lieschen   18f
Giulini, Carlo Maria   36f, 113f
Goldberg, Szymon   145f
Göttingen   19
Graudan, Nikolai   145f
Grimm, Julius Otto   19

Hadow, Sir Henry   14
Haitink, Bernard   36f, 45f, 52f, 68f
Hale, Philip   14
Hamburg   16, 19, 21, 23
Hamburg Philharmonic Society   20, 22
Handel, George Frideric   24, 30,
35, 36, 44

—— Messiah   24, 28
—— Water Music   35
Hanover   18, 19, 21
Harding, H. A.   14
Harrison, Max   135, 178
Haydn, Franz Joseph   25, 26, 32,
52, 115, 144, 174
—— Die Schöpfung   29, 32, 57
—— Piano Sonata No. 62   34
—— Symphony No. 45, "Farewell"   160
—— Symphony No. 80   46
—— Symphony No. 88   25
—— Symphony No. 92, "Oxford"   115
Heidelberg   22
Herzogenberg, Elisabeth von   20, 22
—— Heinrich von   20
Hindemith, Paul   25
—— Symphonic Metamorphoses of
Themes by Weber   25
Horenstein, Jascha   59f
Horszowski, Mieczysław   61f
Horton, John   178
Hotter, Hans   134f
Hungarian Quartet   145f

Indian Music   48
Ives, Charles   38

Joachim, Joseph   18, 19, 20, 22,
26, 54, 163–4
Johnson, Dr. Samuel   22

Kalbeck, Max   178
Karajan, Herbert von   180
Keller, Hans   90
Klemperer, Otto   14, 36f, 180
Kolodin, Irving   46
Krebbers, Herman   68f, 131f
Kreisler, Fritz   131f

Lam, Basil   105
Latham, Peter   117, 135, 138, 177
Leipzig   19, 21
Liszt, Franz   18, 19, 20, 30,
39, 83–7, 89, 90, 109
—— Piano Sonata in B minor   83

Mácal, Zdeněk   140f
MacNeice, Louis   36, 37
Mahler, Gustav   109, 160
—— Symphony No. 6   165

—— Symphony No. 7   119
—— Symphony No. 9   118
Mandyczewski, Eusebius   177, 179
Mann, Thomas   38
"Marks, G. W."   18
Marlboro Festival   32f
Marxsen, Eduard   17, 71
May, Florence   177
Meiningen   22, 118
Mendelssohn, Felix   119, 153
Messiaen, Oliver   38
Milhaud, Darius   14
Monteux, Pierre   14, 36f
Mozart, Wolfgang Amadeus   17, 24, 26,
    34, 115, 118–19, 144
—— *Ein musikalischer Spass* (A Musical
Joke)   55
—— Piano Concerto No. 15, K450   115
—— Piano Concerto No. 21, K467
    145–6
—— Piano Sonata, K533/494   34
—— Quartet No. 15, K421   68–9
—— Symphony No. 39, K543   116
—— Symphony No. 40, K550   25, 57,
    119
Mühlfeld, Richard   22, 118
Mürzuschlag   22

"Neue Zeitschrift für Musik"   19
Neuhaus, Henri   39
Newman, Ernest   14

Orff, Carl   38
—— *Carmina Burana*   38

Palestrina, Govanni Pierluigi da   25, 36
Patzak, Julius   131f
Philharmonia Orchestra   113f
Pierluigi da Palestrina, Giovanni: see
    Palestrina
Porubszky, Bertha   20
Pörtschach   22
Pressbaum   22
Primrose, William   145f
Purcell, Henry   147

Ravel, Maurice   109
Reinick, Robert   128
Reményi, Eduard   18, 19
Richter, Sviatoslav   39
Rimsky-Korsakov, Nikolay   109
Rovetta, Giovanni

—— *Salve Regina*   25
Rubinstein, Artur   180

Sams, Eric   130, 134, 178
Sassnitz   22
Schenker, Heinrich   90
Schlusnus, Heinrich   134f
Schönberg, Arnold   36, 37, 38, 68–9,
    90, 97, 126, 135, 178
—— Variations for Orchestra, op. 31   68
Schubert, Franz   25, 31, 32–4, 37,
    109, 116, 134, 135, 138–9, 140
—— "Wanderer" Fantasy   85–7, 90
—— *Gute Nacht* (from *Die Winterreise*)
    138–9
—— Quintet in C major, D956   33–4
—— Piano Sonata No. 21, D960   33
—— Symphony No. 9, "Great C major"
    118, 125
Schumann, Clara   19–20, 23, 25, 127
Schumann, Robert   14, 19, 26, 90, 116
—— *Zigeunerleben*   25
Senff   19
Serkin, Rudolf   145f
Shaw, George Bernard   14, 82–3
Sibelius, Jean   38, 92
Siebold, Agathe von   20
Simrock, Fritz   21
Singakademie, Vienna   21
Spies, Hermine   20
Stadler, Anton   118
Stockhausen, Julius   21
Strauss, Richard   109, 134f
Stravinsky, Igor   109
—— *The Firebird*   109
Szell, George   113f
Szolchany, George   145f

Tchaikovsky, Pyotr Ilyich   14
—— Symphony No. 5   90
—— Symphony No. 6   160
Telemann, Georg Philipp
—— Overture in C major for three
    oboes, strings, and continuo   57f
"The Times," London   14, 15
Thun   22
Tippett, Sir Michael   38
Toscanini, Arturo   14, 36f
Tovey, Sir Donald   15, 25, 32, 34, 71,
    83, 87, 90, 106, 121, 130,
    139, 178
Trampler, Walter   61f

Van Beinum, Eduard 14
Vaughan Williams, Ralph 160
Vergil (P. Vergilius Maro) 139
Vienna 21, 22, 23

Wagner, Richard 13, 36–7, 83, 109, 141
—— *Walkürenritt* from *Die Walküre*
39
Walker, Alan 89, 90
Walter, Bruno 14

Weber, Carl Maria von 25, 55
Webern, Anton 126
Weimar 18, 83
Weingartner, Felix 14
Wenzig, Josef 135
Westrup, Sir Jack 177
Winsen 18f
Wolf, Hugo 14, 135, 141

Zukerman, Pinchas 61f